Out from Under

Other Outstanding Zenith Books

Four Took Freedom, by Philip Sterling and Rayford Logan. The lives of Harriet Tubman, Frederick Douglass, Robert Smalls, and Blanche K. Bruce.

A Glorious Age in Africa, by Daniel Chu and Elliott Skinner. The story of three great African empires.

Great Rulers of the African Past, by Lavinia Dobler and William A. Brown, with special consultant Philip Curtin. Five African rulers who led their nations in times of crisis.

A Guide to African History, by Basil Davidson, revised and edited by Haskel Frankel. A general survey of the African past from earliest times to the present.

Island in the Crossroads, by M. M. Brau. The history of Puerto Rico.

Lift Every Voice, by Dorothy Sterling and Benjamin Quarles. The lives of Booker T. Washington, W. E. B. Du Bois, Mary Church Terrell, and James Weldon Johnson.

Passage to the Golden Gate, by Daniel Chu and Samuel C. Chu. A history of the Chinese in America to 1910.

Pioneers and Patriots, by Lavinia Dobler and Edgar A. Toppin. The lives of six Negroes of the colonial and revolutionary eras.

The Quiet Rebels, by Philip Sterling and M. M. Brau. Four Puerto Rican leaders: José Celso Barbosa, Luis Muñoz Rivera, José de Diego, and Luis Muñoz Marin.

South by Southwest, by John Tebbel and Ramón Eduardo Ruiz. The Mexican-American and his heritage.

Time of Trial, Time of Hope, by Milton Meltzer and August Meier. The history of the Negro in America from 1919 to 1941.

The Unfinished March, by Carol Drisko and Edgar A. Toppin. The Negro in the United States from Reconstruction to World War I.

Worth Fighting For, by Agnes McCarthy and Lawrence Reddick. A history of the Negro in the United States during the Civil War and Reconstruction.

The aim of Zenith Books is to present the history of minority groups in the United States and their participation in the growth and development of the country. Through histories and biographies written by leading historians in collaboration with established writers for young people, Zenith Books will increase the awareness of minority group members of their own heritage and at the same time develop among all people an understanding and appreciation of that heritage.

DR. JOHN HOPE FRANKLIN, Chairman of the History Department at the University of Chicago, has also taught at Brooklyn College, Fisk University, and Howard University. For the year 1962–63, he was William Pitt Professor of American History and Institutions at Cambridge University in England. He is the author of many books, including *From Slavery to Freedom, The Militant South, Reconstruction after the Civil War,* and *The Emancipation Proclamation.*

SHELLEY UMANS is Director of the Center for Innovation for the Board of Education of the City of New York, a specialist in reading instruction, and a member of the instructional staff of Teachers College, Columbia University. For more than ten years she has been a consultant to many major urban school systems throughout the United States. She is the author of *New Trends in Reading Instruction, Designs for Reading Programs,* and co-author of *Teaching the Disadvantaged.*

JAMES D. ATWATER is a special assistant to the President and was formerly a senior editor for the *Saturday Evening Post* and a reporter and writer for *Time.*

RAMÓN EDUARDO RUIZ is Professor of History at Smith College and author of *The Mexican War: Was It Manifest Destiny?, An American in Maximilian's Mexico, Mexico: The Challenge of Poverty and Illiteracy,* and *Cuba: The Making of a Revolution,* and co-author of the Zenith Book *South by Southwest,* The Mexican-American and His Heritage.

PAUL HOGARTH studied at the Manchester School of Art and at St. Martin's School of Art in London and has exhibited in galleries in London and New York. A descendant of the eighteenth-century English painter William Hogarth, he is the illustrator and author of such books as *Majorca Observed* and *London à la Mode.* He is currently the head of the Department of Illustration at the Royal College of Art.

OUT FROM UNDER

Benito Juárez and the Struggle for Mexican Independence

James D. Atwater

Ramón Eduardo Ruiz, Ph.D.

Illustrated by Paul Hogarth

ZENITH BOOKS

1969/Doubleday & Company, Inc., Garden City, New York

The Zenith Books edition, published simultane-
ously in hardbound and paperback volumes, is
the first publication of OUT FROM UNDER.

Zenith Books edition: 1969

Library of Congress Catalog Card Number 69–12856
Copyright © 1969 by Doubleday & Company, Inc.
Printed in the United States of America
First Edition

CONTENTS

ONE

Village in the Mountains

The village of San Pablo Guelatao lies in the state of Oaxaca in southern Mexico. The region has always been walled off from the rest of the country by great ranges of mountains. Even today, the village is a quiet place. Few tourists bother to journey up through the valleys to seek it out, and those that do find that life there is much the same as it was years ago.

Most of the people who live in Guelatao are Indians. Hundreds of years ago, no one knows exactly when—the ancestors of these Indians founded what is now called Mexico. The Indians of the village, and of all Mexico, are distant relatives of the Indians who lived on the land to the north, which later became the United States. The Mexican Indians are shorter than those in the United States. Their brown skin does not have the reddish tinge of the American Indian.

The Indians of San Pablo Guelatao know little of

what is happening in the world that begins outside the limits of their village. Their entire life belongs to Guelatao, just as their ancestors' did before them, and the life is simple. It is also very hard.

But the Indians of Guelatao have some benefits that are denied the people who live in Mexico's great cities. They can look about them every morning at the beauty of their land. There is a small lake of the deepest blue. The narrow streets are lined by trees. And when the people raise their eyes, there are the great mountains pushing against the sky, so strong and big that they will be standing, just as they stand now, when all of the people and the buildings in the village have disappeared from the earth.

The land endures, and so do the people who feel very close to the eternal beauty of their village. It is part of them, just as the knowledge that they must labor long and hard is part of them.

The hardship of living in the village has forced the people to join together, to be loyal to one another, to form one great family. There are no strangers in Guelatao. Everyone knows everyone else; one person's problems are everyone's problems. Because they are so close to each other, and because they have built a village by themselves without any real outside help, the people of Guelatao are very proud. They are proud of themselves and of their mountains. And they are especially proud of their past. The village of San Pablo Guelatao has known greatness.

On March 21, 1806, an Indian woman named Brígida García, the wife of Marcelino Juárez, gave birth to a

The Mexican people who worked long and hard days on the land felt very close to it.

baby boy in one of the huts of Guelatao. The very next day, members of the family wrapped the baby in the best clothes they could find and carried him carefully to the little church called Santo Tomás Ixtlán. There, in a font that is still used today, the priest baptized the boy Benito Pablo Juárez.

The baby's parents, like all parents, must have hoped that their boy would grow up to become an important man in the village. But it is doubtful that even they dreamed that he would go out into the world beyond the farthermost field of the village. And no one, no one at all, could have guessed that the baby would grow into a man who would change Mexico's history, a man who would be known simply as Juárez. In 1806 Indians in Mexico did not accomplish miracles. Most of them never even learned to read and write. Juárez not only became a scholar. He became a statesman.

Juárez, the little Indian from San Pablo Guelatao, grew up to be the great leader of Mexico in its long struggle for freedom. He took a people who had been held down for hundreds of years by the Spaniards and gave them hope. Juárez fought and won the War of the Reform, a bitter civil war, to give the people a constitution. Later, when France invaded the country, Juárez fought with stubborn determination until he drove the enemy back to Europe and Mexico was Mexico again.

Historians have often compared Juárez to Abraham Lincoln and George Washington. Like Lincoln, he came from humble beginnings. And like Washington, he was the father of his country.

But these comparisons are beside the point. Juárez

was like no other person. Juárez was Juárez. He was an honest politician when this was rare in Mexico. He was the first Indian to rise to a high position in his country. No one who has come after Juárez has faced the same challenges or solved his problems so well. Juárez stands as one of the greatest men in the history of Mexico. He was one of the great men, one of the very great men, of North and South America.

TWO

An Empire Falls

When Benito Pablo Juárez was born in 1806, Spain had owned and controlled Mexico for nearly three hundred years. Spanish rule was much the same as it had been for generations or even centuries. It was complete and it was often cruel. Life in the outside world was changing rapidly, but not in Mexico. Spain had made time stand still in Mexico.

More than twenty years had passed since the thirteen colonies along the Atlantic Coast of North America had joined together and won their independence from England. A small group of Mexicans had followed the progress of the American Revolution with envy. They watched from a distance as the new nation began to grow. They hoped that someday they might be able to break away from Spain in the same fashion. But at the time of Juárez' birth, that hope was still mainly talk and little action.

Today it may seem impossible that Spain could have had such a strong hold on Mexico. After all, Spain was four thousand miles away, and the trip took weeks by sailing ship. But Spain overcame the problem of distance by using harsh methods to turn Mexico into a colony. She managed to control the Indians so thoroughly that they were unable to resist. For example, the Spanish rulers allowed very few Indian children to get an education. And Indians who lived on land owned by the Spaniards often had to work as slaves.

Throughout his career, Juárez would have to struggle to solve problems that went back to the way Spain conquered and ruled the land. Those problems have still not been solved completely. Mexican life today is still being influenced by what the Spaniards did two and three hundred years ago.

The conquest of Mexico by Spain was one of the most remarkable feats in history. When Spain set out to invade Mexico in 1519, only a little more than twenty-five years had passed since Columbus had discovered the New World. The rest of Europe still showed no real interest in putting men ashore to explore the lands across the sea. The English did not set up the colony of Jamestown in Virginia until 1607. The French did not get around to putting an outpost in North America until Champlain established Quebec in 1608. The Dutch waited until 1625 to settle in New Amsterdam, which was to become New York City.

By invading Mexico as early as 1519, Spain got off to a big lead in what was to become a fierce race among the European nations to carve empires out of the New World. This lead was remarkable enough, but it was not the most striking fact about the conquest of Mexico. The fact that still amazes historians is the bravery and skill of the small Spanish armies that fought their way into Mexico. They had no idea what awaited them. Once they set out, they could get no reinforcements from Europe. Spain might as well have been on the moon for all the help it could give them. Everything they needed— food, guns, blankets, clothes—had to be carried, or made, or captured as they went along.

A daring and determined group of adventurers led these small bands of Spaniards. These men conquered not only Indians, but famine and disease. They did not hesitate to kill or to torture to complete the conquest, and complete it they did. They were known as *los conquistadores*—"the conquerors."

The greatest of the conquistadores was the man named Hernán Cortés. Until he took a sword in his hand, Cortés seemed like any other harmless young Spanish nobleman who had left his homeland to seek adventure in Cuba. He was a sportsman and a gambler, but he showed no signs of being a soldier.

Because Cortés happened to work for the governor, he was given command of an expedition to explore the nearby land of Mexico. Cortés, a wealthy young man, used his own money to pay for two-thirds of the cost of his little army—five hundred soldiers, eleven ships, sixteen horses, and ten brass cannons.

This might seem like a pitifully small force to challenge a land as vast as Mexico. But the army's strength had little to do with the number of its men and guns. The army's driving force was the iron will of Cortés himself. The instant he buckled on his armor, a great change came over him. The idle young man became a conqueror.

Cortés was absolutely determined to triumph over anyone and anything that awaited him. He had read the tales of knights winning glory for themselves through feats of valor. Being an imaginative young man, he had been inspired by these stories. Cortés went charging into Mexico like a knight of the Middle Ages challenging a dragon. He was after glory for himself, and if his deeds also brought glory to Spain and to the Catholic Church, so much the better.

When Cortés landed in Yucatán in 1519, Mexico was the home of perhaps as many as three or four million Indians. The richest and the most powerful Indians were the Aztecs. They were far more civilized, in many ways, than any other Indians on the continent of North America, either in the land that was to become Mexico, or the land to the north that was to become the United States.

The Aztec Empire was centered in the Valley of Mexico, which was then known as Anáhuac. The valley lies between two majestic mountain ranges. The air is cool and clear, since the floor of the valley is seven thousand feet above sea level. In the valley the Aztecs built Tenochtitlán, their capital city. Mexico City, the nation's present capital, rises today from the same valley.

Tenochtitlán was as beautiful as any city in Europe. The city was actually built on a number of small islands in Lake Texcoco. As the city grew in size to a hundred thousand persons, the Aztecs drove foundations into the mud at the bottom of the shallow lake and erected build-

9

ings on top of them. Many of the buildings were connected by gardens that actually floated on top of the water. The gardens were planted in giant, wooden frames. The growth of the city spoiled the water in Lake Texcoco for drinking. To get a fresh supply, the Aztecs laid huge, stone pipelines to Chapultepec, which was about four miles away. Three concrete passageways connected Tenochtitlán to the mainland. There was a market place where jewelry, honey, pottery—and slaves—were sold.

While the Aztecs honored beauty, they had little respect for human life if the person happened to be a member of a conquered tribe. Slavery was not the worst fate that a prisoner could receive. He could be killed on an altar of one of the city's forty temples as a sacrifice, which the Aztecs believed would please their gods. The largest temple in Tenochtitlán stood a hundred feet high. It was dedicated in 1487, thirty-two years before Cortés invaded Mexico. The dedication was an event to remember, even by the standards of the Aztecs. According to tradition, twenty thousand persons were sacrificed in celebration. The long lines of victims stretched and wound through the city's streets. Teams of priests dressed in red robes—they did not show the blood—worked steadily to see that the gods were made content.

At the time that Cortés landed in Yucatán, an emperor known as Moctezuma, a name that meant "archer of the heavens," ruled the Aztecs. It was a good name for Moctezuma, for he did seem to have the power of the skies. Tenochtitlán, his capital, was some nine hundred miles from Yucatán. But the Indian Emperor's network of spies and messengers soon sped the word to him that Cortés was ashore.

The Yucatán Indians first encountered by Cortés were easily overcome. Never having seen a horse, they were terrified by the sight of Cortés' men riding on horseback. To the Indians, it seemed as though horse and man were really one creature. They thought that such a fantastic being must be a god.

Moctezuma listened with amazement to the stories about the strange, white-faced men—how they wore metal on their bodies that an arrow could not go through, how they carried tubes that spit smoke and death, and how some of the Spaniards were gods that were half men and half animal.

As Cortés continued to win victories over the Indians, Moctezuma became frantic with worry. Then he had an idea. If Cortés really were a god, as he seemed to be, perhaps he would be satisfied by gifts. If he received enough fabulous presents, perhaps he could be persuaded to stay away from the Valley of Mexico. And so Moctezuma sent Cortés a crown of feathers worn by one of his high priests. He sent bales of cotton, a helmet filled with gold dust, and two huge disks made of gold and silver.

These magnificent presents had an effect upon Cortés, all right, but it was the exact opposite of the one that Moctezuma wanted. They only made Cortés all the more eager to see the Aztec Empire. Cortés boldly burned his ships, so that no man in his army could have any hope of giving up the march and returning home. Then he began the exhausting journey to the Valley of Mexico. It was a bloody march all the way. Some Indian

During the siege of Tenochtitlán, the men of Cortés branded Aztec prisoners and took them into slavery.

tribes greeted Cortés as friends, only to attack him when he was off guard. In his turn, Cortés casually slaughtered large bands of Indian warriors. The young Spanish leader never hesitated to solve a problem with his sword.

Finally, Cortés rode into Tenochtitlán, where the Aztecs greeted him as though he were a god. Moctezuma himself paid him homage. "This palace is yours," he said. But Cortés was not satisfied by this promise. To make sure that the palace—and the city—were his, Cortés kidnaped Moctezuma. Once he had Moctezuma as his prisoner, Cortés ruled the city by forcing the Emperor to issue the orders that he gave him. Then Cortés set out to gather all of the gold and silver he could find. He put aside one-fifth for himself and one-fifth for the King of Spain. The rest was divided among the other members of the expedition.

Cortés kept a strong hold on the Aztecs. At first they were restless, then angry, and finally they rebelled. The Indians' shrieking battle cry echoed through the streets of Tenochtitlán. Cortés forced Moctezuma to try to persuade the Aztecs to stop the attack. But the Emperor's own warriors called him a traitor and stoned him so severely that he died three days later. Greatly outnumbered, but not outfought, Cortés managed to lead his men out of the city and to safety. His little army suffered such casualties that the night of the battle, June 30, 1520, was known to the Spaniards for years as *la noche triste*—"the sad night."

Cortés, of course, refused to accept defeat. He had not gone to Mexico to be defeated, no matter how many Indians he had to face. He retreated to the nearby region of Tlaxcala, where the Indians were his friends and the enemies of the Aztecs. By luck, some Spanish ships arrived in Mexico at this time and the crews decided to join the expedition. Cortés spent months resting his men and repairing his equipment. In the winter he began subduing the Aztec towns around Tenochtitlán and then, in May 1521, he lay siege to the capital itself. For three months, the Aztecs bravely held out. The end came in August. Cortés took command of the ruined city once again and resumed his search for treasure.

In the next few years, the incredible Cortés lived through more than enough adventures to satisfy a dozen knights of the Round Table. But he also began a process that was to become far more important than any feat of arms. Cortés started to change Mexico from a land of many Indian nations into a colony of Spain.

The process began when Cortés discovered that the Aztecs, despite the rumors of their fantastic wealth, really did not have much treasure. Cortés needed some way to stop the grumbling of his men, who had joined the expedition to get rich, and so he divided among them the few gold and silver mines he found. When they still grumbled, he began to give them land—not a few acres, but whole villages.

Then Cortés, a Roman Catholic, sent to Spain for some priests to bring Christianity to the Indians. The Indians turned out to be willing converts, giving up their religion and its tradition of bloody sacrifice. The reasons that the Indians changed so abruptly were simple: they knew that Cortés was a Catholic, and they felt that by adopting his religion they might get some of his power. Also, the Indians really had no choice. To survive, they had to accept the Church of their conquerors. In those

first years, some historians believe, the friars baptized hundreds of thousands of Indians.

Although Cortés did so much to give Spain complete control of Mexico, the Spanish government never allowed him to rule the land himself. The independent spirit that had made him the greatest conquistador of them all had also made him many enemies in Spain. For a few years more, he led other expeditions in Mexico, seeking out new tribes to conquer and to convert to Catholicism, but he never equaled his great campaign against Moctezuma. The King of Spain gave him huge grants of land in Oaxaca. By a coincidence, this was the land that was to produce Juárez nearly three hundred years later. But the gift was not enough to satisfy a man of Cortés' pride. Bitter and alone, Cortés sailed back to Spain.

In the absence of Cortés, the most famous conquistador in Mexico was a man named Francisco Vásquez de Coronado. In 1540 he took three hundred men and went north from the western town of Compostela to find fame and fortune. Coronado found a good deal more fame than fortune. He stumbled onto the Grand Canyon and he explored what is now New Mexico, where he heard some Indians talking excitedly of powerful kings to the northeast. They were said to dine on golden dishes and to nap under trees that tinkled with golden bells. No true conquistador could resist investigating reports like those, and Coronado was a true conquistador. He chased the rumors as far north as the land that was to become Kansas. This was about fourteen hundred miles from Mexico City, a fantastic distance in those days. When he found no golden bells, Coronado finally turned back.

Traveling thousands of miles in search of gold and glory, the conquistadores *conquered the Southwest and converted the Indians to their God.*

Coronado left behind settlements and outposts to maintain the rule of Spain. He also left behind the one prize that the Indians had wanted above all others— horses. The Indians had been eager to get horses ever since they realized that a Spanish soldier and his mount were not one creature. Raiding Indians seized the Spanish horses that Coronado left on the ranches in northwestern Mexico. From these few animals came the herds of horses that the Indians were to use in later generations. They rode them to attack the Mexicans to the south and to fight the settlers who later pushed their way across the plains from the east.

While Coronado was completing the conquest of northern Mexico, Cortés was becoming more and more unhappy in Spain, where he was opposed by the same enemies who had prevented him from being named the ruler of Mexico. He had found that he was a stranger in the country of his birth. Mexico was his true home. After Cortés died in 1547 at the age of sixty-two, his body was taken across the Atlantic a final time and buried, according to his wish, in the convent at Coyoacán.

With Cortés was buried the age of the conquistadores. They had carried the flag, the sword, and the cross throughout the length and breadth of the land. They had conquered the Mexico of the craggy mountains and the high, upland valleys where the air was as sweet as spring water, and they had conquered the Mexico of hot, treeless plains where the force of the sun could drop a man from his horse. After the conquistadores, Mexico would never be the same again.

THREE

Under Spain's Thumb

Spain's intentions toward Mexico were at first a curious mixture of greed and good will. The Spanish King and his rulers seem to have wanted to help improve the life of the Indians. But Spain also looked upon Mexico as a source of wealth that could be loaded on board ships and taken back to Europe.

The two aims soon began to conflict. Spain discovered that it could not at the same time help the Indians and take away everything they had that was of value. When Spain learned it could do one thing or the other, but not both, the country lost no time in deciding which one to pick. Spain chose to take the wealth and to stop caring about the Indians. From the time of the conquistadores until Juárez was a teen-ager—a span of three hundred years—Spain owned and treated Mexico like a colony.

To rule Mexico in his name, the King of Spain named a man who had the title of viceroy. His word was law. Next in power to the viceroy, who was always a Spaniard who had been born in Spain, were the men called the *gachupines,* a word meaning "those who wore spurs." This was a reference to the Spanish conquistadores who had come riding into Mexico on horseback. All gachupines were born in Spain. These gachupines brought Spanish brides to Mexico and raised families, but a strange thing happened to their children. Since they were not born in Spain, they were not gachupines. They did not have the influence of their fathers and mothers. The children born in Mexico of Spanish parents were known as *Creoles.* As time went on, their number grew steadily larger. These Creoles naturally resented the fact that they were not allowed to hold the top posts in the government, which were reserved for the gachupines. Even more the Creoles resented the fact that they were doomed to a second-class position in everything they did. The gachupines were always holding the better jobs, owning the bigger ranches, controlling the richer mines. As the centuries went by, their discontent would grow increasingly bitter until it became a major factor in the stormy history of the country.

If the gachupines and the Creoles agreed upon any one thing, it was that the Indians should be held down. They should not be allowed to become educated, or to get good jobs, or to acquire wealth. The Spaniards knew that if the Indians were allowed any liberty, they would naturally want more. And the more they got, the more they would always want until there would be a danger of a mass uprising. To prevent this, Spain worked out a system of controlling the Indians that was so thorough that its influence is still being felt today.

The Spanish system of controlling Mexico was one of the most extreme examples in history of what is known as "colonialism." This was the practice by which an advanced country, such as Spain, took possession of an underdeveloped land and turned it into a "colony." The mother country would then increase its own wealth and power by controlling the people and the resources of the colony.

To one degree or another, all of the big European nations practiced colonialism in the last half of the nineteenth century, or the first half of the twentieth. In every case, native leaders in the colonies came to hate the control of the mother country and to want freedom for their people. After World War II, many colonies in Africa and Asia demanded and won their liberty from their European leaders.

Spain gave the viceroy complete political power in Mexico. His word was law. But Spain's colonialism in Mexico went far beyond the power of the government. The control was also military, economic, and religious. The army, which was led by the gachupines, patrolled the country as though it were a defeated enemy nation. The Indians were treated with contempt.

By far the greatest hardship suffered by the Indians was the fact that the Spaniards forced them to work as slave labor. The enslavement took many forms. In some areas, the Spaniards divided the land among themselves into what were called *encomiendas*. Any Indian who happened to live on the land would have to work for his Spanish master or risk death. The Spaniards who had been given gold or silver mines by the conquistadores could force the Indians to work for them. The Creoles steadily expanded their ranches by simply taking over the lands of the neighboring Indians and then getting the government to make the theft legal. As these ranches grew to huge sizes, they became known as *haciendas*. In time, they absorbed most of the good farming land in Mexico's valleys.

With few exceptions, the Catholic Church did not try —or was unable—to help the Indians, although they were devout worshipers. For one thing, the King of Spain was also head of the Church. He was unlikely to let the priests help the same Indians that he was trying to hold down.

As time went by, the Catholic Church grew steadily richer. Church officials became owners of their own haciendas. They took over whole sections of city property. In fact, the Church became so successful in business that it controlled much of Mexico's money. Poor as they were, the Indians had to pay taxes to the Church. The great cathedral in Mexico City gained an altar of solid silver and an altar rail that shone with gold.

One of the main reasons that the Catholic Church got so much power in Mexico was that it did not have to obey the colony's laws. The law that applied to everyone else just did not apply to the Church. A Catholic priest could be tried only by the Church's own system of courts. This privilege was called the *fuero*. The Creoles and the Indians alike came to despise it.

While colonialism was a careful plan to keep the Indians poor and uneducated, the Spaniards brought with them to Mexico, completely by accident, one of the most effective weapons to break any power the Indians might have. That weapon was disease. The Indians had never known smallpox or influenza in their entire history. Their bodies had no defenses against either sickness. Time and time again, great epidemics swept through Mexico, killing Indians by the tens and even the hundreds of thousands. Although the Indians always had lots of children, the diseases killed so many people that their numbers actually declined for generations after the age of the conquistadores.

The Spaniards did not mean to control the Indians with disease, of course, but they did plan a number of other ways of keeping them under their thumb. No matter how smart an Indian child might be, he or she had next to no chance of getting an education. By the 1790s, shortly before Juárez was born, there were only a few grade schools in the entire colony. And even if an Indian boy were lucky enough to learn how to read and write, it would do him no good. No Indian could become a doctor or a lawyer. He seldom could become a priest, no matter how religious he might be. All he could do was to work with his hands. And yet he was handicapped in even this kind of a job. If he were a farmer, for example, he seldom had a horse or planted European crops. He did not even use a European plow.

Under these harsh rules, the Indians soon lost all of the learning and skills and culture that they had built up in the days of the Aztecs. In fact, the Indians seemed to go backward in time. After a few generations of Spanish rule, most Indians were worse off than their ancestors had been a hundred years before. Their bed, a *petate*, was a straw mat that was spread on the hard ground.

The Spanish sold the Indians' land and then forced them to work on it as slaves.

Their food was corn and beans, which they raised by scratching furrows in the dirt with pointed sticks. Their huts were often made of clay.

And so the centuries slipped quietly by. The gachupines, arriving from Europe every generation, kept their power and kept getting rich, and the Creoles also grew richer. By the time of the American Revolution, Mexico City, which rose on the site of Tenochtitlán, had turned into the biggest and certainly the gayest city in the New World, surpassing New York, Boston, and Philadelphia. There were bullfights and fancy dress balls. Every day at 5 P.M. the wealthy ladies put on their newest dresses made from the silks of China and rode up and down the handsome avenues. The men, in turn, dressed up in their silk jackets and bright blue riding pants that sparkled with silver buttons. They pulled on their biggest silver spurs. Then, mounted on horses with saddles and bridles that gleamed with silver, the cavaliers rode out to parade in front of their ladies.

It was a handsome sight—one that would have graced the streets of Madrid or Barcelona back home in Spain. But there was also a kind of forced gaiety to the scene, as though the actors and actresses knew it could never last. As the eighteenth century came to a close, a new race of people was gaining power in Mexico. These people were called *mestizos*. They were the result of marriages between Indian women and Spanish men that had taken place in Mexico since the arrival of the first conquistador. As time went on, the mestizos began marrying each other, and so the race that was part Indian and part white grew rapidly.

Because they had Indian blood, the mestizos were treated nearly as badly as the Indians themselves. Naturally, the mestizos came to hate both the gachupines and the Creoles. By the start of the nineteenth century, some of them were angry enough to be thinking of rebelling. But the Spaniards were still too strong and, more important, the mestizos did not have a leader. It was still too early for the person who would lead them to victory. It was 1806, and the Indian named Juárez had just been born.

FOUR

A Leader Appears

There was a good reason why the family of Benito Juárez had the baby boy baptized the day after he was born, instead of waiting a week or so as is now the custom. His parents were afraid that he would sicken and die before he could be made a Christian. Like all of the Indian villages of Mexico, Guelatao was at the mercy of disease. Juárez, in fact, was only three years old when his entire life was changed by sickness. Both of his parents died, and he was left to be raised by an uncle named Bernardino.

Uncle Bernardino had not married, so the little boy had no mother, and he grew up in a home without any brothers or sisters. This was very hard, of course, but in some ways his uncle was a fine guardian. Uncle Bernardino was the man who first inspired Juárez to get an education. The uncle himself was not an educated man,

Benito Juárez learned to read from his uncle who encouraged him to get an education.

but he did know how to read some Spanish, which was a rare skill for an Indian in those days. He taught young Juárez how to read. Years later, when Juárez had become famous, he wrote an account of those early lessons for his children. He had wanted to learn so badly, Juárez recalled, "that when my uncle called me to give me my lesson, I myself brought him the whip to punish me if I did not know it."

But his uncle was not able to satisfy Juárez' craving to learn. As he grew older, Juárez appears to have become unhappy living with his uncle. He had to be a shepherd boy, spending long hours out alone with his animals in all kinds of weather. The experience of being on his own so much helped give Juárez the characteristics he would use so well in later life. He became patient and industrious, and most important of all, self-reliant. For want of a better audience to instruct, he would climb a tree and lecture his flocks. He had to speak in his native Indian tongue of Zapotec, since he did not know any Spanish.

While Juárez was talking to his sheep, great events were beginning to stir in Mexico. It is unlikely that the boy knew of them, or that anyone in the village knew of them, for that matter. And it is certain that if the news somehow reached Guelatao no one would have guessed that the events were part of a movement that eventually would involve the little shepherd boy who lived with Bernardino. Slowly, very slowly, Mexico was starting down the road to independence.

The chain of events that was to give Mexico its independence actually began in Europe as far back as the life of a British philosopher named John Locke, who died in 1704. Locke argued that all men have the same natural rights, that no man has special rights because he has a lot of money or is born to a wealthy family. All men should be equal under the law, and no man should be ruled by anyone else unless he had agreed to the system.

During the eighteenth century, these basic ideas developed in many forms that were known by the general name of "liberalism." The ideas were revolutionary for, at that time, the kingdoms of Europe were based on a totally opposite belief—that some men had more rights than others. These men formed the nobility, and at the head of the nobility was the King himself. The kings claimed that God had given them the right to rule others. The kings of Spain, for example, used this belief to justify their control of Mexico. Spain, it was argued, was simply superior to Mexico, and that was that.

While the spirit of liberalism was growing in Europe, the British colonies in North America were beginning to adopt the ideas of the movement. The colonies argued that England had no right to rule them, since they had not agreed to the system and did not have a voice in it. In 1776 the colonies' demand for their rights produced the Declaration of Independence, written mainly by Thomas Jefferson, which became one of the world's great documents of liberalism. In the second paragraph, Jefferson wrote, "We hold these truths to be self-evident, that all men are created equal, that they are endowed by their creator with certain unalienable rights, that among these are life, liberty, and the pursuit of happiness. That to secure these rights, governments are instituted among men, deriving their just powers from the consent of the governed. That whenever any form of government becomes destructive to these ends, it is the right of the people to alter or abolish it, and to institute new government . . ."

From 1775 to 1783, the people of the colonies fought the American Revolution to abolish the "destructive" rule of England and to "secure these rights" by instituting a new government, the United States of America.

In 1789, the ideas of liberalism helped touch off the great French Revolution against the most powerful kingdom in Europe. The bloody overthrow of the French throne changed the course of European history. The people had risen up and seized power. When the revolution began to lose its force, a soldier named Napoleon Bonaparte took control of France in 1799.

The rest of the world remembers Napoleon as a brilliant general who nearly succeeded in conquering all of Europe. Mexico remembers him as the man who invaded Spain in 1808 and forced King Charles IV and his son, Ferdinand VII, to leave the country. Napoleon put his brother, Joseph Bonaparte, on the Spanish throne.

The defeat by Napoleon left Spain powerless to control most of her great empire in the New World. To the south of Mexico, native leaders seized the chance to rebel against the mother country. Simón Bolívar and José de San Martín were two of the men who led the fight that established many of the countries of South America as they are known today.

In Mexico, meanwhile, the leaders of the mestizos had watched with fascination as the series of tremendous events shook Europe. According to the ideas of liberalism, Spain had no right to rule Mexico. The Mexicans had neither agreed to the system, nor did they have a voice in it. In the past, some Creoles had been as harsh on the mestizos as the gachupines, but now the leaders of the two groups were drawn together by the ideas of liberalism. Yet they were unable to decide how to organize a revolt against the gachupines and Spain. When the revolt did come finally, in 1810, it happened almost by chance, and the man who led it was an unlikely revolutionary, His name was Miguel Hidalgo y Costilla, and he was a priest.

A highly educated man, Father Hidalgo was very familiar with the ideas of liberalism. In fact, the Church had stationed him in the little, out-of-the-way town of Dolores because of his disturbing ideas and his plans to help the Indians. In 1810, during the debates over what action Mexico should take against Spain, Father Hidalgo joined a number of Creole leaders in his region who were plotting a revolt against the gachupines. When the plan was discovered, the army set out to arrest the plotters, but Father Hidalgo decided not to flee. Instead, he boldly decided to start the revolt then and there. "Come on, Valleza," he told a companion, "you are going to arrest the gachupín priests." He turned to his brother. "And you, Mariano, will arrest the gachupín traders."

So began the Mexican War of Independence. It was an incredible idea. There was no organization, no planning. There was only a bold, determined Catholic priest who felt that justice would win, no matter what, and suddenly there was an army of fifty thousand Indians and mestizos and a few Creoles following him. Father Hidalgo proclaimed the independence of Mexico and the equality of all its people. This document became known

Father Hidalgo's demands for justice and equality led to the revolt of the people against Spain.

as the *Grito de Dolores*. *Grito* means "cry" in Spanish, and Dolores was the name of the priest's village. For the next hundred years, the Mexicans would fight to reach Father Hidalgo's goals of independence and equality.

The gachupines had the army on their side, but Father Hidalgo had men who wanted nothing more than to kill a Spaniard. Most of the Indians had no idea how to fight a modern army. Some of them were equipped with little more than knives and clubs. Some of them tried to put the Spanish cannon out of action by throwing their sombreros over the muzzles.

But the strange army of revolutionaries won some mighty victories, and for a while it seemed that nothing could stop Father Hidalgo. The gachupines were terrified. Mexico was being turned upside down before their eyes, and they knew they would be on the bottom.

Then Father Hidalgo made the same kind of quick, bold decision that had begun the revolution in the first place. He decided to march out to end the war by fighting one decisive battle at a bridge called Calderón. His troops were holding out well until luck went against them. Wagons filled with ammunition caught fire. The dry grass began to blaze. Suddenly Father Hidalgo's Indians and mestizos found themselves under attack from the gachupines from the front and by fire from the rear. It was too much for the Indians. They broke ranks and ran, and with them went the revolution.

Father Hidalgo escaped, but he was seized a few months later when one of his men betrayed him. The gachupines ordered him to be shot. The firing squad put Father Hidalgo in a chair. The story goes that when he saw how nervous the soldiers were he tried to help them by pointing to his heart. It did little good. The soldiers were so upset at having to shoot a priest whose name had become a rallying cry that they fired three volleys without killing him. Finally, in desperation, they placed the muzzles of their guns right against his body and so ended the life of the man who had nearly freed Mexico. The gachupines hung the heads of Father Hidalgo and three of his generals from a public building in the city of Guanajuato.

The revolt did not die with Father Hidalgo. One of his followers, a priest named José María Morelos, kept up the fight. Although he himself was a Roman Catholic priest, Father Morelos insisted that the Church should not be allowed the privilege of the fuero—freedom from any laws except those of the Church itself. Father Morelos also declared that the Church should be forced to give up its lands. He argued that the Indians should have equal rights with the gachupines, and he said that the great haciendas owned by the Creoles and gachupines should be split up and given to the Indian and mestizo peasants. In fact, Father Morelos went so far as to argue that all of the property of the very rich should be seized and divided equally between the government and the poor.

The army finally caught Father Morelos in 1815. They sneaked him out of the City of Mexico so that none of his followers could find him. Then they shot him. That ended the actual military operations of Mexico's War of Independence, but it did not end the revolution. The movement begun by the two Catholic priests had frightened the gachupines and it had inspired the Creoles, the mestizos, and thousands of Indians. The Mexican leaders who followed the two priests realized that they owed them a great debt. A Mexican historian named Justo Sierra has said, "You had to hear Juárez say 'el señor Morelos' to understand the extraordinary tradition of devotion that the men of the generation that followed that of the insurgents received from their fathers."

At the time that Father Hidalgo and Father Morelos were shaking Spain's grip on Mexico, Juárez was still a shepherd boy in his little mountain village of a hundred persons. Still, an inner force seemed to be driving Juárez, even at that age. He craved an education. Finally, in December 1818 the desire became too great for him to resist. He left his uncle's home one day and walked the forty-one miles to the state's capital of Oaxaca. He had no money. He was twelve years old, but he was on his way.

War Breaks Out

By luck, young Juárez happened to have a sister named María Josefa in Oaxaca. She worked as a cook for a dye trader named Don Antonio Maza, who agreed to take in the young Indian boy until he found a place to live. Three weeks later, Juárez had more good luck. He was adopted by exactly the right kind of man. Don Antonio Salanueva was a bookbinder and a scholar. He was also a kind man whose heart went out to the barefooted, solemn, little Indian boy with the serious black eyes. Don Antonio eagerly agreed to make Juárez his son and to give him the very best education he could get in Oaxaca.

Juárez turned out to be a fine scholar and a devoted son to the bookbinder. He plunged into his studies like a swimmer who is suddenly given a chance to dive into the ocean after being confined to little mountain pools. There is a story that a neighbor woman gave him a piece of rosin, which burned like a candle, so that he could read late into the night. But life in the city was not all study for Juárez. He was a wiry, agile boy who could usually beat his friends in a race or in jumping contests. Once he designed a diving board at a lake near the city. He tested it himself—and did a belly flop into the water when it broke. But after a friend suggested some changes, the diving board worked fine. Juárez charged his friends three or four cents a jump, and then took all the money he had earned and bought fruit candy for the whole gang.

While Juárez, without knowing it, was preparing for his career as the leader of Mexico, his country was continuing to change rapidly. When the gachupines shot Father Hidalgo and Father Morelos, they postponed the revolution, but they did not stop it. The mestizos still wanted to break free of Spain and so did many Creoles. The Indians who had fought by the side of the two martyr priests had realized for the first time that they could actually stand up to the hated Spaniards.

All of these groups were ripe for revolution when an event took place in Spain that was to change the history of Mexico. The year was 1820. Napoleon had been crushed for four years. The armies of England and Prussia had defeated him once and for all in 1815 near the little Belgian town of Waterloo, which gave the famous battle its name. Without the help of his brother Napoleon, Joseph Bonaparte had been unable to hold power in Spain, and Ferdinand VII was back on the throne.

Ferdinand VII did his best to jail Spain's liberals, but he did not quite succeed. In 1820 the King was about to send an army to South America to restore Spain's control of the countries that had been freed by Bolívar and San Martín when some liberal soldiers started a mutiny. Other liberals staged riots throughout Spain. Thoroughly alarmed, Ferdinand VII agreed to adopt a constitution that gave the people many rights they did not have before.

Following these events from Mexico, the Creoles suddenly became worried. They were afraid that the same liberal constitution would be given to their colony. If that happened, the Creoles knew that the constitution would help the mestizos and the Indians so much that they might someday take control of the government. The Creoles, who were not liberals, wanted to take over the government themselves.

The history of Mexico is a history of plots to gain— or seize—power. The Creoles worked out a plan in 1821 that was one of the most cunning of them all. They decided that they must free Mexico from Spain. That would stop the constitution from going into effect. Once Mexico was independent, the Creoles were gambling that they could keep the mestizos and the Indians in check.

To put the plan into effect, the Creoles used a handsome, young general named Agustín de Iturbide. He had been the commander of the troops that had shot Father Morelos. Iturbide, a Creole, seized control of the government, and Mexico declared itself free from Spain.

It was very quick and very simple, and for a while the whole country rejoiced. Then the mestizos and the Indians realized that they had been betrayed. The Creoles let the Catholic Church keep all of the privileges

that had caused so much hatred and bitterness among the people.

The Creoles also set up what they called the Mexican Empire. As king, the Creoles had hoped to get a member of a European royal family. They had even hoped that perhaps King Ferdinand VII would take the throne. But General Iturbide saw his big chance. Since he controlled the army, he simply made himself Emperor. Everything was just about the same as it was before 1821. The only difference was that the throne that ruled Mexico was inside the country instead of in Europe.

For the next hundred years, the history of Mexico was to be a constant struggle for power between the mestizos and the more daring Indians on one side and the Creoles on the other. During the next thirty years or so, the struggle would weaken Mexico so much that Spain might easily have regained control of her former colony were it not for the stand taken by England and the United States. In 1823 President James Monroe declared that any interference by European powers in the affairs of North or South America would be opposed by the United States, a declaration accepted by the powerful British government.

The struggle for the control of Mexico is one of the most confusing chapters in the history of the New World. It will help to keep in mind that, basically, the struggle was a fight between the liberals and the conservatives. The liberals were inspired by the ideals of equality that were expressed in the American Declaration of Independence and in the French Revolution. Most of the liberals were mestizos—the class that had been held down by the Spaniards since the days of Cortés.

To help the masses, the liberals knew that they would have to break the power of the ruling class. This was made up mostly of Creoles, the gachupines, the Church, and the army. The Creoles and the gachupines had their differences but more things united them than divided them. They were especially united by the fear that the country would someday be controlled by the liberals.

The members of the ruling class were called conservatives. Just as their name suggests, they wanted to conserve things. They wanted life in Mexico to stay just the way it was, with themselves on top and the mestizos and the Indians on the bottom. The friends of the conservatives were called the reactionaries. They reacted to liberalism by becoming even more conservative than the conservatives. They wanted things the way they were in about 1600.

How much the young Juárez knew of the conservatives and the liberals and such matters as the Monroe Doctrine is not known. He was growing up in Oaxaca, a sleepy little town of about twenty-five thousand people, even though it was the capital of the state of the same name. It is known that Juárez had problems of his own during this period. Even in the schools of Oaxaca, he was not learning as much as he wanted. Don Antonio and the boy discussed the matter for long hours. Juárez had noticed that many bright boys his age were attending the Catholic seminary in town. They were training to become priests. Juárez was a deeply religious Catholic, as were most of the Indians of his time, but he had no inner desire to become a priest. Yet he decided that he wanted a good education so badly that he would like to attend the seminary anyway. The church in Oaxaca was one of the few that would allow an Indian to become a priest. Juárez' new father, who had always wanted him to become a priest, happily agreed to the plan. The boy entered the seminary in 1821.

The plan did not work out well. Juárez discovered that he could not fool himself—he just did not have enough interest in the Church. He was soon bored by the religious subjects. Then, in 1827, Juárez had another piece of good luck. A liberal movement in the state set up a new college in Oaxaca. Juárez left the seminary and began his education all over again.

Juárez was still attending college in 1829 when a great event occurred in Oaxaca. A general named Antonio López de Santa Anna arrived to attend a banquet. The college students acted as waiters and, completely by chance, Juárez served Santa Anna. The general would never forget the quiet Indian padding back and forth from the kitchen in his bare feet. Years later, the two men were to become bitter enemies. In fact, much of the history of Mexico would be shaped by the growing rivalry between the two men. But on the night of the banquet, Santa Anna seemed far too famous and too powerful for anyone to bring down, let alone an Indian boy in bare feet.

Of all the sly schemers in the history of Mexico, Santa Anna was the master. He spent a lifetime plotting to gain power. Sometimes he won, sometimes he lost, but he always carried on in high style. Santa Anna never did anything in his life that was drab. Everything was

Technicolor. He changed sides as easily and as often as he changed his gaudy uniforms. But he always kept two goals in mind: he wanted to rule and he wanted to stop the liberal movement from changing Mexico. Santa Anna was a prize example of the reactionary. He reacted to the liberals by trying to halt progress. He would have liked to rule Mexico as though it were one big hacienda filled with slaves and servants.

Santa Anna was still a teen-ager when he had fought as an officer against the Indian troops of Father Hidalgo. He matured into a moody, palely handsome man with the natural air of command of a leader. They say his voice could bellow an order above the roar of cannon, or charm a lady with a whisper.

In 1821 Santa Anna had helped Iturbide, his senior officer, become Emperor. Then, hungry for power himself, he turned around and helped drive him out of office that same year. Emperor Iturbide was succeeded by a liberal named Guadalupe Victoria, who became Mexico's first president. But Victoria was a poor leader and Mexico drifted. In 1834 Santa Anna seized the capital and made himself dictator. He dismissed the congress and put the key of the building into his pocket.

While Santa Anna was rising to power, trouble was beginning to brew in the vast, northern area of Mexico known as Texas. The region was about the size of France, the soil was rich, and it was nearly empty of people, except the fierce Comanche warriors. Texas was such an attractive prize, in fact, that in the 1820s the Mexicans began to worry that the rapidly growing United States would be bound to try to seize it someday. As a barrier to the United States, the Mexicans decided to set up colonies of their own in Texas. The problem was the lack of people to settle there. As a solution, Mexico made very generous offers of cheap land to any citizens of the United States who would agree to live in Texas and to accept the duties of Mexican citizenship.

Between 1825 and 1830, some fifteen thousand people from the United States crossed the border to live in Texas. So many came, in fact, that the Mexicans began to worry that Texas was really becoming a kind of colony of the United States, although the people were supposed to be Mexican. In 1830 Mexico declared the border closed to any more citizens of the United States. This act made the Texans furious. They felt that they should continue to grow by getting more people from the United States. The Texans asked the Mexican government to open the border and allow them to set up their own state. Mexico said no to both requests. But Mexico was powerless to stop more people from illegally crossing the border from the United States into Texas.

In 1834, after he had become dictator, Santa Anna sent a small army into Texas to enforce the law. The Texans decided to fight. In December 1835 they defeated the Mexicans in San Antonio. When he heard the news, Santa Anna himself gathered together an army of three thousand and marched into Texas in February 1836. He found a hundred and fifty Texans waiting for him in an old San Antonio mission known as the Alamo. For ten days the Texans held out against Santa Anna. Then, finally, the Mexicans overran the little garrison. Santa Anna's bugles sounded the *degüello,* a call that dated back to Spain's bloody wars against the invading Moors hundreds of years before. The call meant, "Kill all the defenders." And the Mexican soldiers did. Among the defenders who died were Jim Bowie, who supposedly invented the big Bowie knife, and Davy Crockett, the frontiersman.

As it turned out, Santa Anna won a battle and lost a war. The men of the Alamo became heroes not only to the Texans, but to all people in the United States. "Remember the Alamo!" became one of the most famous battle cries in history. Six weeks later, the Texans under Sam Houston surprised Santa Anna at San Jacinto and routed his forces. When he was captured, Santa Anna was dressed as spectacularly as ever—blue cotton jacket, linen trousers, cap, and red slippers.

After defeating Santa Anna, Texas became a separate republic and soon began to press for annexation to the United States. At the time, Texas had only about seventy thousand settlers, and the leaders of the new republic were afraid that Mexico, a nation of seven million, would try to recapture its huge colony. In 1845 the United States Senate finally voted to annex the territory. The new addition was so vast that it included not only the land that was to become the state of Texas, but an area that was to provide about half of New Mexico and small portions of Kansas, Colorado, and Wyoming— territory explored so long before by Coronado.

In 1838, just two years after his defeat in Texas, Santa Anna got his chance to ride back into power. Some celebrating Mexican soldiers had damaged a bakery owned by a Frenchman. France demanded payment for the damages, but the Mexicans refused. Suddenly the two countries were fighting what was called *La Guerra de los Pasteles*—"the pastry war." It was a kind of cream-puff war, limited to raids on the Mexican coast by a French fleet, but it served Santa Anna's purposes. He galloped into Veracruz one day just as a French raiding party was heading back to its ships. Before departing, the French fired a cannon loaded with grapeshot at Santa Anna. The general had the good luck to be hit. His right leg was hurt so badly that it had to be amputated, which naturally made the Mexican people feel sorry for him. But Santa Anna also told everyone how he had driven the French into the sea, just to make the story better. Suddenly he was a hero.

Five years later, in 1843, the general again became President of Mexico. He had his amputated leg dug up and reburied as a kind of national relic in the cathedral in Mexico City. He also began comparing himself to Napoleon.

These years are known in Mexican history as the "Age of Santa Anna" because the general dominated them so completely. No one knows how many times he held the presidency. Some say six—some say eleven. He and his rivals were constantly throwing each other out of office. The method they used was called the *pronunciamiento*. A group of officers would seize the government and then pronounce—or announce—that it was ruling.

One of the finest and liveliest accounts of Mexico during these years was written by a Scottish school teacher who married a Spanish diplomat named Angel Calderón de la Barca. Señor Calderón was Spain's ambassador to Mexico at this time, and Señora Calderón excitedly described the country in her letters. One of her best tells of a revolt against the President, who at the time was Anastasio Bustamante.

"Revolution in Mexico! or Pronunciamiento as they call it," she writes. "The storm which has for some time been brewing has burst forth at last. Don Valentín Gómez Farías and General Urrea have pronounced for federalism. At two this morning, joined by the fifth battalion, they took up arms, set off for the palace, surprised the president in his bed, and took him prisoner. Some say it will end in a few hours—others, that it will be a long and bloody contest. Some are assured that Santa Anna will come on directly and [take] the presidency.

"The firing has begun! People come running up the street. The Indians are hurrying back to their villages in double-quick trot. All the streets near the square are planted with cannon. All along the street people are standing on the balconies, looking anxiously in the direction of the palace."

While the Age of Santa Anna was progressing, the person who was to become the general's great enemy was quietly changing from a boy into a man. Juárez finished college in 1831 and became a lawyer in Oaxaca. Two years later he began his political career as a deputy in the Oaxaca state legislature. He had none of the dash of Santa Anna—and none of the dishonesty. He was a small man, standing only a little over five feet tall, and he wore clothes that were almost always black. His career did not soar like a skyrocket, but he made steady progress at a time when few Indians held any office in Mexico.

In 1843 Juárez married Doña Margarita Maza, the daughter of Don Antonio Maza, the man who had first taken him in when he came to Oaxaca. It was quite an accomplishment for an Indian to marry the daughter of a distinguished Creole. Juárez' wife, who was only seventeen, reportedly said of her husband, "He is very homely, but very good." They would have twelve children, seven girls and five boys. Four of the boys and one girl died.

In 1847 Juárez was appointed governor of the state of Oaxaca. The Mexicans call 1847 "the terrible year," and with good reason. It was a year of war with the United States, a war that was to cost Mexico a huge slice of its territory. The bitterness caused by the war in Mexico against the United States was to last for years.

The United States calls the conflict the Mexican War, and historians are still arguing about its causes and who was to blame for the beginning of the fighting. Those who feel that the United States began the war claim that it was caused by the ambitions of President James Knox Polk. He seemed to believe, as did many Americans at the time, that the United States had the right to control North America from the Atlantic to the Pacific. In fact, some citizens of the United States felt that God had given them that right. The idea that the United States must grow until it reached from sea to shining sea was called Manifest Destiny, and it was to influence U.S. foreign policy for the rest of the century.

The problem with Mexico was that it stood in the way of Manifest Destiny. The annexation of Texas, of course, had helped push the United States a long way toward the Pacific, but Mexico still owned what was

In 1847 a war broke out between Mexico and the United States. The war left Mexico with bitter feelings toward the United States.

then known as California, although at the time it included far more land than what was eventually to become the state of that name. Spanish explorers had claimed for the King a vast area stretching from the Pacific through what is now California, Nevada, Utah, Arizona, and parts of Colorado and Kansas. When Mexico broke free of Spain, it inherited all of these lands. The great expanse of Mexico blocked the United States and President Polk from the Pacific.

In November 1845 President Polk had sent John Slidell of Louisiana to Mexico as his representative to offer to buy California. But the Mexicans would not deal with Slidell because of their resentment against the United States, which still lingered from the annexation of Texas. Many Mexicans were convinced that the United States had secretly encouraged settlers to go into Texas with the idea of causing a revolt against Mexico and then joining the Union.

At the time of Slidell's mission, the Mexicans were also arguing with the United States over the rightful boundary of Texas. The Mexican government argued that the Nueces River was the legal southern border, a claim that could be justified by the history of the territory. The United States, on the other hand, insisted that the real border was the Río Grande, which is far to the south of the Nueces.

After the Mexicans refused to bargain with Slidell over California, President Polk sent a force under General Zachary Taylor across the Nueces. Taylor, who had been fighting Indians for forty years, was known as "Old Rough and Ready." Spoiling for a fight, he set up camp along the Río Grande itself. To the Mexicans, Taylor was nothing less than an invader of their territory. On April 25, 1846, a band of Mexican cavalry crossed the Río Grande and killed some U.S. soldiers.

That little skirmish gave President Polk his excuse to declare war, if he had been looking for one. "Mexico has passed the boundary of the United States, has invaded our territory, and shed American blood upon the American soil," Polk said. "War exists, and, notwithstanding all our efforts to avoid it, exists by the act of Mexico herself."

The struggles of the previous thirty-seven years had left Mexico exhausted. The country was no match for the young and vigorous United States. But Santa Anna did the best he could. Somehow the old campaigner gathered together an army and marched out to meet the Americans. It was probably his finest hour, although it was a losing one. General Taylor defeated him at the Battle of Buena Vista on February 23, 1847. After sending Taylor south, President Polk made sure of getting California by sending General Stephen W. Kearny with a small force on a march from Missouri to the Pacific. Then General Winfield Scott, known as "Old Fuss and Feathers" for his vain manner and colorful uniform, landed at Veracruz with twelve thousand men and marched on Mexico City. Two of the young officers in Scott's army were to become famous on other battlefields in later years. Their names were Ulysses S. Grant and Robert E. Lee. In the late summer of 1847, Scott attacked the Mexican capital. Santa Anna, realizing all was lost, agreed to surrender.

It had been a short, ugly war. No one gained much glory except, perhaps, the young Mexican cadets. Although they were only boys, they fought bravely during the defense of Chapultepec outside of Mexico City. Refusing to surrender, some of the boys jumped from the cliffs to their deaths.

The settlement of the war gave the United States all of the territory between the Río Grande and the Pacific Ocean, an area bounded on the north by what is now the southern border of Oregon. With one short war, President Polk had managed to make the Manifest Destiny come true.

The end of the war left Mexico in great confusion once again. Many old rivals were beginning to fight to win control of the government. Santa Anna fled south and sought refuge in the state of Oaxaca. But Juárez, the new governor, would not admit him. He feared that war, which always followed Santa Anna like his shadow, would come with him. Juárez wanted Oaxaca to stay neutral.

Juárez' decision infuriated Santa Anna. From that moment on, the two men were enemies. Wondering why Juárez had turned him away, Santa Anna later wrote, "He could not forgive me because he had waited on me at table in Oaxaca, in December 1829 with his bare feet on the floor and in his linen smock and trousers. It is amazing that an Indian of such low degree should have become the figure that we all know."

It was natural for Santa Anna to search for a personal motive to explain what Juárez had done. Actually, Juárez merely wanted to preserve the peace in his state. He was anxious to begin using the ideas of liberalism to improve the lives of the people of Oaxaca.

People Demand Reform

As the governor of Oaxaca, Juárez was a figure of somber dignity—black suit, black bow tie, black cane—but his programs were fresh and imaginative. He built roads, reduced the state's debt, and erected schools by the hundreds. He wanted the children to be given the education that he had been forced to struggle for.

Juárez' first term as governor was one of the happiest times of his life. He was helping Indians and mestizos who had suffered for hundreds of years. He also had time at home to play with his children. Juárez' one moment of deep grief during this time came in 1850 when Guadalupe, his two-year-old daughter, died of cholera. True to the Indian custom, the governor himself shouldered the tiny coffin and carried it to the cemetery.

Then, like a cat with nine lives, Santa Anna reappeared in Mexico City in 1853 and rode back to power as President. At the time, Juárez had finished his term

57

Juárez spent his happiest days as governor of Oaxaca, where he was able to help the Indians and mestizos *get an education and live a better life.*

as governor and was working as a lawyer. Santa Anna did not take long to seek his revenge on his old enemy. Juárez was arrested on a trumped-up charge of trying to turn the people of his state against each other. For a while, Juárez was held in the ancient stone prison of San Juan de Ulloa, which was in the harbor of Veracruz. He was released in 1854 and ordered out of the country. He chose to live in New Orleans because a small colony of Mexican rebels had settled there.

It was a time of great sadness for Juárez. He missed his family deeply. When a ship was due to arrive from Mexico, Juárez would be waiting on the pier hours before it docked if he thought it might be carrying a letter. Although he was a skilled lawyer, he did not speak English well enough to practice. He had to take any job that came along. At one point, he rolled cigars to get enough pennies to buy coffee and black bread.

But in many ways, the long night of exile was good for Juárez. He had time to think about Mexico's problems. He became the trusted friend of the other Mexican liberals in the city. The most important of these leaders was a man named Melchor O'Campo. Like Juárez, O'Campo had been a former governor of a Mexican state.

During the months in New Orleans, the little group of rebels became a kind of liberal government in exile. They believed all men were equal and that the government should help them get their rights. They read and discussed the writings of José María Luis Mora, the Mexican they regarded as the "father" of liberalism in their country. In the meantime, Santa Anna was up to

60

his old tricks at home. He was ruling Mexico as a dictator. He condemned to jail or exile anyone who opposed him. He spent money so foolishly that Mexico was nearly bankrupt. And Santa Anna had lost none of his love for personal glory. He insisted that he be addressed as the "Most Serene Highness."

In a country that had been given a glimpse of liberty, there was bound to be an uprising against Santa Anna sooner or later. It came in February 1854. The leader was a tough old soldier named Juan Alvarez. He had been fighting for liberal causes ever since he had campaigned as a young man for Father Morelos.

General Alvarez succeeded. It was Santa Anna's turn to go into exile. In 1855 Alvarez became the new President and filled his cabinet with many of the men who had been planning in New Orleans for just such a day. Juárez became the minister of justice.

So began what is known in Mexico as "The Reform." In the next few weeks, Juárez was able to begin the programs he had planned in New Orleans. At the time, the Church still enjoyed the privilege of the fuero, which had always been bitterly resented by the people. Juárez was able to put through a decree, known as the *Ley Juárez*. (*Ley* means "law" in Spanish.) The Ley Juárez restricted the fuero. In some matters, but not all, the clergy would have to stand trial in the nation's regular system of courts, just as everyone else did. The time was not yet ripe for Juárez to remove all of the privileges of the fuero. The Church still had too much power.

The proclamation of the Ley Juárez made the author greatly loved by the liberals and greatly hated by the

Juárez and other liberal exiles in New Orleans planned for the day when they could return to Mexico.

conservatives, who wanted things to stay as they were.

Later Juárez backed another decree designed to break the Church's tight control on the state. This one, which was called *Ley Lerdo,* put the Church's lands up for sale. This move, of course, was fought by the Church and the conservatives, and approved with enthusiasm by the liberals. In 1857 Juárez was listened to with respect when the liberals called a convention to write a constitution for Mexico. The aims of both leys were written into the constitution of 1857. In addition, the document went one big step farther. It gave the government control over the Church. In its other passages, the constitution set up a form of government much like the one that rules the United States.

The uproar that followed the adoption of the constitution confused Mexico's bewildering political life even more. Angered by the new liberal legislation, the conservatives had solidified their opposition to the government, which was now in the hands of President Ignacio Comonfort, who had replaced Alvarez. The old warrior had resigned soon after taking office. Juárez, however, had remained in the new administration as minister of justice who, in the Mexican political system, was also vice-president.

Soon the conservatives were plotting to overthrow President Comonfort. Juárez knew of the plan—in fact, everyone knew of the plan. The newspapers even wrote about it. But Juárez did nothing, really, to try to stop what was known in Mexico as the *golpe de estado*— "the seizing of power." Because of this, some persons in the government suspected he was in on the plot. As the vice-president, Juárez would have succeeded Comonfort as President if he left office. Juárez' reputation with the liberals was saved by the fact that he was arrested by the new government. This obviously meant he had no part in overthrowing President Comonfort.

When he was let go a few weeks later, Juárez had become the most famous liberal in the country. This was the time when the little Indian's stubborn will power and utter self-confidence really began to show. He decided to form a liberal government as a rival to the conservative. He would try to save the constitution. But this time he would not go to New Orleans. This time he would form the government in Mexico. O'Campo would be his foreign minister.

Juárez slipped out of Mexico City and set out for the liberal stronghold of Guanajuato about two hundred miles to the north. He walked much of the trip. One night he slept in the fields, just as he had done as a shepherd boy years before. When he got to the small city of Guanajuato, he declared the establishment of a constitutional government. Then he began raising an army. Thus began the War of the Reform, a full-scale civil war, one of the bloodiest of all the bloody Mexican wars.

It was a war, basically, between the liberals, such as Juárez, and the conservatives. Both the Church and the regular army supported the conservatives. The liberals wanted to change Mexico to give the masses of people a better life. The conservatives wanted Mexico to stay just the way it was, with themselves on top and the people on the bottom.

Juárez was certain that he was right. He was certain that right made might. And he was certain, therefore, that he was bound to win. When his little army was routed by the conservatives at the Battle of Salamanca, Juárez said calmly to a friend, "Our cock has lost a feather."

But Juárez' troubles were only beginning. A few days later, some of his own troops revolted against him. They ran through the corridors of his headquarters shouting, "Long live the Church! Long live the army!"

Juárez and his staff were thrown into a cell. After two days soldiers decided to shoot them. A squad of men burst into the cell and raised their rifles. Their leader shouted the commands: "Ready! Aim!" Juárez calmly grasped the cell door and raised his head. Suddenly one of Juárez' aides, an emotional poet named Guillermo Prieto, threw himself in front of his President just as the officer shouted: "Fire!"

The soldiers were confused by Prieto's action. They did not shoot. Prieto cried, "Put down your guns! Brave men are not murderers!" The soldiers were so impressed by Prieto's display of bravery and loyalty to Juárez that they spared the lives of all the men in the cell.

The event became one of the most famous in Mexican history. It is the best example of the strong feelings that underlay the long struggle of Mexico to become a nation. Many of the Mexican leaders were emotional men. Their moods could change very rapidly, just as the mood of the firing squad had changed in an instant. Yet Juárez, above all others, controlled his feelings. His diary has only a single line about his brush with death: "On the 13th the guard of the palace mutinied and I was taken prisoner. On the 15th I was set free."

Soon after this incident, Juárez' troops suffered an-

other defeat. The entire army that was left was made up of three hundred and fifty soldiers and two cannons. Juárez decided to move his headquarters to the port of Veracruz. There he could get help from the sea.

The war continued to go badly for the liberals, but Juárez, feeling sure that he would win, outlined the reforms he planned to put into effect when he gained victory. Once again, most of his reforms concerned the Church. He declared that all Church property, except the church buildings themselves, should be taken over by the government. For years Juárez had been against the Mexican system that made Catholicism the official religion of the country. This was the old European custom. Non-Catholics could not worship as they pleased. The Church also became an ally of the government. Because the Church wanted to keep its privileges, it naturally had a conservative influence upon the government.

Juárez declared that Church and state should be separate, just as they were in the United States. He said that Mexico should not have an official religion. Anyone should be able to worship in any way he saw fit. This right, known as "religious liberty," is a basic part of the Constitution of the United States.

Juárez' decrees formed the Reform Laws. They gave the liberals a program to win the support of most of the Mexican people. But Juárez controlled only the city of Veracruz. Before he could carry his reforms to the rest of the country, he would have to win the war. And the war was becoming a nightmare.

All of the hatred between the various classes of Mexicans that had been building up for generations was spilling over. In many ways, the conflict was a religious war.

Prieto threw himself between his president and the soldiers. This brave action saved Juárez' life.

The liberals and the conservatives were fighting over the place of the Church in Mexican life. All wars are terrible, but religious wars are often the worst. They arouse fierce emotions on both sides. The soldiers fighting in Mexico's civil war performed feats of great bravery and of great cruelty.

Both sides slaughtered the innocent. Men were dragged from their homes and shot before the horrified eyes of their wives and children. Great areas of Mexico were ruled by army units that often acted like bands of outlaws. Mexico seemed to be slowly bleeding to death.

In Veracruz, President Juárez struggled with overwhelming problems. He was constantly afraid that a European country would take advantage of Mexico's weakness and try to make a colony out of the young nation. Worse yet, there was always the threat that the United States would seize the chance to take more of Mexico's territory. In 1858 President James Buchanan actually asked Congress for the power to take over two Mexican states called Sonora and Chihuahua that adjoined Texas and the region that was to become Arizona and New Mexico. Buchanan argued that the United States had the right to take control of the states because the property of U.S. citizens in Mexico was being damaged by the war. Congress refused to allow Buchanan to go ahead with his scheme, but Juárez never knew when the spirit of Manifest Destiny would again move the United States to try to carve out another chunk of Mexico for itself.

As the war dragged on, Juárez became desperately short of supplies and money. The conservative army actually surrounded Veracruz. Shells screamed across the city and burst in the streets. In one week, they killed thirty-eight women, men, and children. The liberals' situation seemed hopeless. Some of Juárez' own cabinet ministers began urging him to make peace with the conservatives.

Juárez refused. The Indian from the village of San Pablo Guelatao had fought too long to give up. The war turned into a contest of endurance. The side that could accept the most suffering would win. It was as simple as that.

Juárez was used to suffering. He did not break. Conservative President Miguel Miramón did. On the night of December 23, 1860, Juárez and his wife were attending the opera in Veracruz when a messenger galloped up to the theater. Juárez glanced through the letter that was pressed into his hand and ordered the curtain lowered. Then, quietly, he read aloud the news. The liberal army, under General González Ortega, had won a great victory at Mexico City. The war was over.

On January 11, 1861, Benito Juárez entered the capital in triumph. He was President of all Mexico.

A Nation in Name Only

Although Juárez had won the civil war, Mexico was still a nation in name only. The country lay exhausted after the long and bitter struggle that had been going on for more than fifty years, ever since 1810, when Father Hidalgo had begun his revolt. The bitterness that had caused the civil war still remained. Juárez controlled the capital, but he did not control vast sections of Mexico. Bandits and groups of conservative soldiers terrorized the people in the countryside.

Juárez learned just how badly his country was torn within weeks of taking office. Don Melchor O'Campo, Juárez's old companion from New Orleans, had retired from the government and was living quietly with his family near the capital. One day a band of conservative soldiers seized him. Juárez tried to save his friend by arresting some conservative soldiers as hostages, but it did no good. O'Campo was too big a prize for the raiders to let go. They put him on his horse and made him ride out into the countryside. When he was told to halt, O'Campo dismounted and gave his last possessions to the members of the firing squad. He found a peso for the bugler. Then the soldiers shot him.

The death of his friend was a shattering personal blow to Juárez. What was more, it also showed how powerless the President was to act. The soldiers had held O'Campo prisoner for four days within easy riding distance of Mexico City.

To capture the killers, Juárez promptly sent out a group of his best soldiers under a liberal general named Santos Degollado. Juárez was still in mourning for O'Campo when General Degollado blundered into an ambush and was killed. Juárez then ordered General Leandro Valle, another of his best leaders, to take up the search. A few days later General Valle was also ambushed and killed by the enemy.

Juárez fought back the only way he knew. He vowed to himself that he would hold on to the government, come what may. If winning the peace was to be a contest of endurance, just as the civil war had been, then Juárez was prepared to endure.

During these months Juárez held the liberal government together with sheer will power. An Englishman named Charles Lempriere, who watched Juárez address congress during those troubled days, described him as a "dark, small man, quiet and self-possessed." Lampriere added, "He is affectionately known in Mexico as the 'little Indian.'"

At one point, Juárez' problems became so heavy that he was driven to an act that he hated. He suspended some of the constitutional rights of the people so that he would have a freer hand in dealing with the rebel groups. This decision enraged some of Juárez' own liberals. A total of fifty-one liberals in congress signed a paper asking the President to resign. The little Indian merely set his jaw and worked harder.

Juárez had other problems to worry about. The long war had cost so much money to fight that Mexico was nearly bankrupt. There was barely enough cash to keep the government going. To make matters worse, Britain, France, and Spain began insisting that Mexico repay the debts the country had piled up during the past years. Juárez did the only thing he saw he could do. He stopped all payments of foreign debts—and soon found himself in the midst of the gravest crisis of his career. Europe once again was thinking of seizing Mexico.

The plotting had actually begun years before. Various conservative groups in Mexico wanted a European power to take over the country. They wanted Mexico to be made into a kingdom, controlled from Europe, that would restore all of the privileges of the upper classes. Creole, gachupín, and church leaders had all proposed the idea. In 1854 none other than Santa Anna had sent a man to make the rounds of the European courts. The messenger was unsuccessful, and Santa Anna was forced to stay in exile on an island in the Bahamas.

A few years later, another wealthy conservative tried his luck in Europe. His name was José Manuel Hidalgo y Esnaurrizar. He happened to be a casual friend of a lady known as Eugenie. She was the wife of Napoleon III, the Emperor of France. Napoleon III had a long, waxed mustache and a plump belly, which he held in with a corset. He was lucky enough to be the nephew of Napoleon Bonaparte himself. Although he was a weak man, the power of his uncle's name helped him become the ruler of France.

One summer night in 1861, the Empress Eugenie was bent over her embroidery when a servant announced that a Señor Hidalgo had asked if he might speak to her. She was delighted to chat with the dashing, charming Mexican, and she forgot all about her embroidery as he outlined his plan. Eugenie was a lady of action. She wasted no time. She brought Napoleon III into the room and said to Hidalgo, "Tell the Emperor what you have just told me."

What Hidalgo proposed to Napoleon III that night was this: Send an army to Mexico, take the country, set up a kingdom, and put a European of royal blood on the throne. Hidalgo assured Napoleon that Juárez and his meager forces were too weak to stop the might of France. He pointed out that the Civil War had just begun in the United States—there was no need to worry about U.S. intervention despite the Monroe Doctrine, which said that the Union would oppose any European move into the hemisphere. Hidalgo promised Napoleon that the Mexican people hated Juárez and his ideas. He said that Mexico would welcome the French soldiers as their liberators.

Napoleon was delighted by the idea. He thought it would bring France some power and himself some glory. It so happened that both Spain and England were planning to send small military forces to Mexico to persuade Juárez to pay his nation's debts. Napoleon joined them. But the British and the Spaniards only wanted to

Forced to leave Mexico City by the French, Juárez lowered his country's flag and cried out, "Viva México!"

threaten Juárez. When he came to an agreement with them, they quickly got back on their ships and sailed away. Not Napoleon. He was after a bigger prize.

In the spring of 1862, Napoleon sent a well-trained army of six thousand professionals into Mexico. To his astonishment, they were not greeted as heroes by the people. Still, the French were totally confident. Their general wrote home, "We are so superior to the Mexicans in race, in organization, in discipline, in morality, and in elevation of feeling, that at the head of six thousand soldiers I am already master of Mexico." Ten days later, Juárez' ragged but tough soldiers badly defeated the boasting general. His honor hurt, Napoleon sent in another army of thirty thousand. Juárez was forced to abandon Mexico City once again. He stood on the roof of the National Palace as the flag was lowered. When it was down, the flag was given to him. He raised it to his lips and cried out, "Viva México!" The crowd shouted back, "Viva México!" And then the President of Mexico headed for the safety of the north.

In the meantime, Napoleon III had decided upon the man he wanted to put upon the Mexican throne. He was a twenty-nine-year-old Austrian nobleman named Maximilian, the third amazing and contrasting personality of these stormy years of Mexican history. The first, of course, was Juárez, the stubborn, solemn liberal. The second was Santa Anna, the scheming, aging reactionary. If anything, the young Austrian was an even more unusual individual than either Juárez or Santa Anna.

Maximilian was the brother of Austria's Emperor Franz Joseph. He had a flowing blond beard, which was frequently combed by a manservant, since the owner was accustomed to the better things of royal life. Maximilian had his dreams of glory, but he also had become sympathetic to liberalism. He yearned to improve the lives of the peoples of the world. But, as a nobleman, Maximilian was also very much a member of the ruling class. The effort of trying to be a liberal made the young nobleman a very confused person.

When the Mexican throne was offered to him, Maximilian was fascinated by the idea. He imagined how much good he could do for all those poor Mexicans. But, like all weak men, he had trouble making up his mind. The person who finally persuaded him to take the throne was his wife, Carlotta. She was a fiercely ambitious woman who wanted power for her husband and herself.

Maximilian became convinced that the people of Mexico wanted him as much as he wanted the throne. He even wrote to Juárez suggesting that the Indian leader might like to join his new government. The astonishing letter shows how little Maximilian knew about Mexico or about Juárez. There is no record of the Mexican President's reply. At the time, the Indian leader was retreating into the mountains to the north. Once again, he was preparing to fight it out as long as necessary.

Nor did Maximilian have any idea how much the United States was against Europe's return to the New World. He was even encouraged by a pledge of support from the Confederacy in 1863, although the pledge was meaningless. That was the year the South lost the battles of both Gettysburg and Vicksburg, and with them any chance of winning the war. The offer of help, interestingly enough, was made by John Slidell, the South's representative in Paris and the same man who had gone to Mexico in 1845 to try to buy California for President Polk. Although he was deeply occupied with the Civil War, Abraham Lincoln had kept a worried eye on the French invasion of Mexico. "I don't like the looks of the thing," he said. "Napoleon has taken advantage of trouble and has attempted to found a monarchy on the soil of Mexico. If we restore the Union, I propose to notify Louis Napoleon that it is about time to take his army out of Mexico. When that army is gone, the Mexicans will take care of Maximilian."

Even if Maximilian had heard Lincoln's warning, it is unlikely that he would have paid attention to it. He was lost in his dreams of the glory he would find in Mexico and the good he would do there. In the spring of 1864, he set sail for the New World. To pass the time aboard ship, he began writing a six-hundred-page manual of court etiquette. It was one of the few subjects he did know something about. If he was to be an emperor, he would rule like an emperor, and he would be treated with the proper respect due an emperor.

Maximilian and Carlotta landed in Veracruz on May 28, 1864. There were no cheering masses to meet them. There was no one to meet them at all. The great misadventure had begun.

EIGHT

An Emperor for Mexico

A day later, the Mexican conservatives finally did send someone to meet the man who they hoped would save them from Juárez. As the long journey began to Mexico City, Maximilian and Carlotta looked expectantly for the welcoming crowds of their devoted subjects. There were none, of course, although some Indians did greet them with enthusiasm. Curiously enough, there was an old Indian legend that told of a blond, bearded leader who would come to them from the East. Some Indians thought that Maximilian must be the man in the legend.

The Austrian's dream that Juárez would become his ally popped within a day or so. Juárez sent Maximilian a letter that fairly quivered with anger. A man like Maximilian, Juárez wrote, might have the power "to attack the rights of others, seize their goods, assault the lives of those who defend their nationality, make of their virtues crimes, and one's own vices a virtue, but there is one thing beyond the reach of such perversity: the tremendous judgment of history."

Juárez' letter dismayed Maximilian but he did not feel discouraged. He felt certain that he would win. Meanwhile, the Mexican conservatives were hard at work to make it seem that history was on the side of Maximilian. They carefully arranged a great celebration in his honor to greet him and Carlotta as they rode through the gates of Mexico City. A young Mexican named José Luis Blasio, who later became Maximilian's private secretary, wrote about the scene. "There were hundreds of open carriages filled with the most distinguished and beautiful women of Mexican society, escorted by men in formal attire. Under the clear blue skies, crowds milled about carrying tricolored banners, leafy branches, and countless bouquets of gay flowers."

The next day Maximilian and Carlotta took part in a great procession that must have made them think that the throne of Mexico was as royal as any in Europe. Blasio wrote that the Emperor and Empress were escorted by the army's finest cavalry. Sixty carriages carrying Mexican officials followed the imperial coach. "The sovereigns went first to the cathedral where a solemn *Te Deum* was chanted, and after this ceremony they walked to the palace in the midst of a multitude of more than a hundred thousand persons who filled the air with their deafening applause."

On that day, Blasio got his first look at Maximilian. "I saw him pass, arrogant, majestic, and well-proportioned. Above all I was impressed by the mildness of his expression which later it was my privilege to contemplate so many times. His long, golden beard, parted in the center, gave him such an aspect of majesty that it was impossible to see him without immediately being attracted and fascinated."

Maximilian and Carlotta were utterly convinced by the demonstrations arranged by the conservatives that they really did command the loyalty of the country. They were overwhelmed by the beauty of their new empire. Maximilian used to love to stand high in the palace and gaze out over the Valley of Mexico and the great mountains beyond. It was a land fit for an emperor, and Maximilian, young, romantic, and inexperienced, was foolish enough to believe that he was fit to be its emperor.

He began the most absurd projects. He carefully wrote out a set of regulations for the navy he planned to build for Mexico. It made no difference that Mexico did not have enough money to build a rowboat. In Europe, every great power had a navy, and so Maximilian made his plans. He dreamed of extending his empire down into South America. He convinced himself that the Indians adored him. He even wrote proud letters home about how far advanced Mexico was over Europe.

Once he had the throne, Maximilian lost no time acting like an emperor. He ordered an artist to start painting a series of seven portraits of himself. In six months, Maximilian and Carlotta gave seventy lunches, twenty banquets, sixteen balls, and twelve receptions. In one year, he spent a hundred thousand dollars of Mexico's dwindling treasury on wine. The Mexicans were soon puzzling over Maximilian's elaborate rules of court etiquette, which would have confused a French

Maximilian as Emperor of Mexico had seven portraits painted of himself.

prince. When Maximilian once decided to make a trip by water, he traveled in a large canoe that was so elaborate that it had carpeting over the floor boards. Supper was served at midnight. Maximilian and his guests drank champagne.

But as time went on, Maximilian in some ways began to act as though he were not the Emperor at all. He felt such a strong bond with the Mexican people—"my people"—that he began to dress like them, and to eat ordinary *frijoles* and *tortillas*. This display of democratic feeling in the Emperor they had so carefully put on the throne bothered the conservatives, but the worst was yet to come. To the horror of his supporters, Maximilian turned out to be something of a liberal. His motto, which he had embroidered on tapestries, was "Equity in Justice." This seemed to mean that justice made every man equal—an idea that Juárez himself would have applauded.

The conservatives began to wonder if they had made a friend or a foe in the Emperor of Mexico. Maximilian became disgusted with the greed of some Catholic clergymen in the country. "The clergy are lacking in Christian charity and morality," he said. He also grew to dislike the conservatives in his cabinet because they were always scheming for power. He was repelled by his generals' custom of casually shooting liberal prisoners. To correct these evils, Maximilian began making laws that he assumed would be carried out once they were announced. The conservatives let him write whatever he liked; they had no intention of putting such laws into effect. But they were shocked when their Emperor ordered a system of schools to be built and abolished the

83

Juárez fleeing farther and farther north was forced to retreat to a town close to the Mexican-U.S. border.

old practice of peonage—a custom that amounted to slavery for farm workers.

Then, on December 27, 1864, Maximilian really proved that, at heart, he believed in many of the same things as Juárez. The Emperor issued a decree that adopted most of the restrictions on the Church that Juárez had ordered years before. Maximilian had managed to enrage the two main groups that had brought him to power—the clergy and the conservative politicians.

Still innocent, Maximilian thought that now perhaps Juárez would be willing to join his government. The Emperor sent a messenger to the Indian President, along with an autographed picture of himself. Juárez was as outraged as before. He scorned the proposal and commented, "The clergy are now disgusted with Maximilian, who has betrayed them by adopting in effect the laws of the reform." Juárez stated, "When a foreigner intervenes in our affairs with his bayonets, we shall make war on him to the death."

For a man in such a desperate condition, it was a brave cry. Juárez had been forced to go deeper and

84

deeper into the north to escape the French armies. His little procession was pitifully small compared to the great parades and squadrons of cavalry that accompanied Maximilian wherever he went. Juárez and a few friends rode in a battered carriage. Behind them followed a second carriage that contained all of the important papers of the liberal government. The entire liberal movement was carried in those two carriages and in the mind and heart of the little Indian in the dusty black clothes. One night the conservative soldiers made a surprise attack on the caravan. During the wild gallop to safety, bullets ripped through Juárez' carriage.

Juárez was made to retreat to the little town that is now known as Ciudad Juárez, which is right on the Mexican-United States border. He was more than a thousand miles from Mexico City. He was too short of money to buy munitions. He was not sure which of his liberal generals he could trust. After the long years of struggle, they were beginning to look for power for themselves. He was opposed by thirty-five thousand French troops, the match of any in Europe. He was terribly alone. His wife and family were refugees in New York. During their long separation, two of their sons had died. The news almost drove Juárez to his knees. He rarely showed his emotions, but his few friends knew how heartsick he was after so many years away from his family.

And yet Juárez would not quit. He had outlasted other rivals, and he was sure he could outlast the strange young man with the blond beard and the fuzzy liberal ideas who perched anxiously on the throne of Mexico.

As Juárez endured poverty and discouragement in the north, the tide slowly began to turn against Maximilian. On April 9, 1865, General Robert E. Lee surrendered the Confederacy to the Union's General Ulysses S. Grant at Appomattox Courthouse in Virginia. The two rival generals had campaigned together in Mexico twenty years before. The end of the war had a strong and immediate effect upon the contest between the determination of Juárez and the dreams of Maximilian. President Lincoln was assassinated within a few days of the end of the war, but his successor, President Andrew Johnson, was just as eager to force the French out of the New World. With the South defeated at last, the Union was able to re-establish the basic idea of the Monroe Doctrine—that no European power would be allowed to meddle in the affairs of North or South America. President Johnson warned Napoleon III that his support of Maximilian was endangering the friendship of France and the United States.

To make the point absolutely clear, Johnson sent General Philip Sheridan, the great Union cavalry commander, to the Mexican border at the head of an army of a hundred thousand veterans, the finest troops in the world. If they crossed the border, they could drive the French into the sea. Supplies of arms were made available to Juárez' troops.

Across the Atlantic, Napoleon III nervously read the reports of how the United States was determined to throw his forces out of Mexico. Napoleon, a born loser, had assumed that the Confederacy would win the Civil War. The fact that the United States was now threatening an attack was bad enough, but Napoleon had even worse problems in Europe. Prussia, France's ancient enemy, was arming for war. After one last attempt to crush Juárez failed, Napoleon III decided to give up. He sent word to Maximilian that he was pulling out of Mexico. He said that he hoped the Emperor would leave with the troops.

The news, of course, astounded Maximilian. Everything had seemed fine to him as he gazed about his little empire with misty-eyed affection. In fact, he had just sent off another misguided letter to one of Juárez' aides. Speaking of the President, Maximilian had said, "If, as I believe, he really desires the good of Mexico, he must soon see that no Mexican has such warm feelings for his country and its progress as I, and that I am working with the utmost good will and honesty; so let him come and help me faithfully and sincerely, and I will receive him with open arms, as I would any good Mexican."

When he got the news that the French were leaving, Maximilian for once showed some common sense. He decided to go with them. But the Empress Carlotta was not ready to face reality. She appealed to her husband's pride to stay. He agreed. He also agreed to let her go to

Europe in 1866 to plead with Napoleon to maintain his support of the empire.

Carlotta found Napoleon ill and completely concerned with Prussia. Three times she pleaded for his support. Napoleon listened, wept with sympathy, and said no. The refusal had a strange effect upon the Empress. She began to have wild dreams that Napoleon was the Devil himself and was trying to poison her orange juice.

Carlotta next journeyed to Rome to try to get help from the Pope. There she was joined by the faithful secretary Blasio, who had been sent across the Atlantic by Maximilian to take care of her. Blasio noted in his diary, "She wore deep mourning, a cloak of black velvet and a small bonnet with black silk ribbons tied under her chin. We could see that her face was haggard, her eyes sunken, and her cheeks blazing—symptomatic of the intense fever that had consumed her in recent days."

The Pope received Carlotta politely, but he refused to help Maximilian. The Emperor, after all, had taken away the special privileges of the Church in Mexico. At this rebuff, Carlotta's mind collapsed altogether. She told the Pope that Napoleon was trying to kill her. "Kneeling before the Pope and sobbing, almost shrieking," wrote Blasio, "she implored him to protect her."

Carlotta finally agreed to go to a hotel. There, with only a maid to attend her, she lived the life of a madwoman. Trusting no one, she went into the street herself to get water. The maid prepared all of the meals because the Empress feared that Napoleon was still trying to poison her. Carlotta even had live chickens brought into the elegant hotel room. She tied them to the legs of a table.

After a while, Carlotta's brother came to Rome and took her home to Belgium. She was hopelessly insane. The Mexican empire might have been made of colored paper and ribbon, but she had believed it would last forever. When it collapsed, she collapsed. She never saw Maximilian again.

When Maximilian heard the news of his wife, he again decided to give up the throne and return to Europe. But then he learned that Austria might not welcome him home. At the same time, the Mexican conservatives begged him to stay. They would be helpless before Juárez if both he and the French left. Maximilian hesitated for six weeks, as he always did when facing a decision. Then he agreed to stay. It seemed to be the honorable thing to do. When the last French troops marched out of Mexico City on February 8, 1867, Maximilian watched from behind a curtain in a window of the palace. "At last I am free," he said.

Then Emperor Maximilian placed himself at the head of a few thousand conservative troops and marched out to decide his fate—and Mexico's—in open battle with Juárez.

The National Chief

Juárez was ready and waiting to do battle with Maximilian. A short time before, he had barely escaped an attempt by one of Maximilian's armies to capture him. While he was visiting the city of Zacatecas, a number of imperial soldiers suddenly attacked. The President's own aides were actually firing point-blank at the enemy when Juárez finally galloped to safety.

The liberal forces rallied and later destroyed the army that had come so near killing their leader. With the victory, Juárez knew that the war was drawing to a close. He welcomed the supplies from the United States. Every day he could see his army of lean, hard veterans growing stronger.

Juárez knew of Maximilian's troubles and Carlotta's unhappy journey. The President also knew that the French were abandoning their puppet Emperor. But there is no hint of boasting in Juárez' letters about how he would triumph over Maximilian. It was not a time for gloating. Juárez had come too far and seen too many men die to gloat. Besides, Juárez was not the kind of man who could celebrate the troubles of another, even if the other man was his rival for the control of Mexico.

And so the final act of the contest between the strong-willed Indian and the emotional Austrian nobleman began very quietly. Juárez' army was too tired to strut. And this time Maximilian rode out of Mexico City without his escort of dashing French cavalry officers.

Blasio tells how Maximilian insisted upon living like a soldier. He slept on the ground at night in a roll of blankets. He was marching with nine thousand men toward the conservative stronghold of Querétaro, about a hundred miles north of Mexico City. During lulls in the march, Maximilian dictated changes in his book of court etiquette. He had to believe that there would still be a court when the fighting had ended. Trying to act like a soldier, Maximilian exposed himself to the fire of the liberal troops that raided the column of march.

Maximilian's courage brought about a touching little scene described by Blasio. "On March 20, Maximilian organized a military celebration in the plaza of La Cruz. He stood under a tent decorated with flags and flowers and, to martial music and the roar of cannon, bestowed decorations and medals on the officers and men who had distinguished themselves in the recent fighting. When he had finished, Miramón (a conservative general) approached and in a short and affecting speech asked permission to confer upon him one of the medals of copper given to privates for bravery. Maximilian was deeply moved and embraced Miramón after the general had affixed the medal to his uniform and expressed thanks."

Once they reached Querétaro, Maximilian and his army were soon surrounded by some twenty-seven thousand liberal troops. Maximilian, still confident that he had some power, sent a messenger to Juárez with a request that they begin bargaining. The President would not even speak to the man.

Maximilian set up his headquarters in a convent in the city. He refused to listen to any schemes for getting away. As the siege went on, Maximilian seemed to want to be killed in action to save his honor.

Before dawn on May 15, 1867, the liberal army overran the city and invaded the convent. Maximilian managed to flee the building with some of his generals. One of his aides said he had found a perfect place for the Emperor to hide in. "Hide?" asked Maximilian. "Never!"

A short while later, Maximilian and his little group were surrounded. Maximilian said, "Let us get on our horses and try to get through. If we cannot get out, we can at least die in the attempt."

But one general, who did not worry as much about his honor as the Emperor, said, "There is nothing to do but surrender."

An officer walked toward the liberal soldiers carrying a white flag made from a sheet. The war was over. Juárez had won. The soldiers on both sides stared at the flag of surrender for a few seconds before they understood what it meant. They had been fighting for so many years that it did not seem possible that the war could end in one moment. When they realized that the bloodshed really had stopped, they fired their muskets into the air with joy.

The question remained of what was to be done with Maximilian. The Emperor asked to be allowed to return to Europe. He swore "never to interfere in Mexican politics again." Juárez refused the plea and ordered Maximilian to stand trial. In his cell, Maximilian still worked on his manual of etiquette—he never gave up hope—and listened intently to the conversation of his guards. But the Emperor had never learned enough Spanish to understand what they were saying about his chances. When the trial began, Maximilian haughtily refused to attend it.

He was sentenced to death. There was little else the court could do. In 1862 the liberals had passed a law condemning to death anyone who plotted against Mexican independence. Maximilian obviously was guilty of that crime.

Even so, there was a wave of sympathy for the foolish Austrian who had been talked into believing that he could rule Mexico. Even the United States suggested to Juárez that he treat his old enemy mercifully. A lady from an old Mexican family went so far as to throw herself at the President's feet. She hugged his knees and begged for Maximilian's life.

The answer that Juárez is said to have given her sums up all the thoughts that had been running through his mind about his duty to his country. "I am grieved, madam," he said, "to see you on your knees before me, but if all the kings and queens of Europe were at your side, I could not spare his life. It is not I who take it away; it is my people and the law, and if I did not do their will,

Although some Mexicans begged for Maximilian's life, Juárez said no. "It is not I who take it away; it is my people and the law."

the people would take his life as well as my own."

The cruel truth of the matter was that Maximilian had to be shot. Both the Mexican law and the Mexican people demanded it, as Juárez said. The act would be the strongest possible warning to Europe not to interfere in Mexico again. It is one of the saddest tragedies of Mexico's long fight for freedom that Maximilian had to be sentenced to death. He may have been a dreamer, and he often acted like a fool, but at heart he wanted many of the same reforms for the Mexican people that Juárez wanted himself.

On June 19, 1867, Maximilian was dressed in black and driven out of the city in a carriage. Four thousand soldiers and a firing squad were waiting for him on the plains nearby. When Maximilian stepped out of his carriage, he looked up at the fair blue sky and said, "I always wanted to die on a beautiful day like this."

The former Emperor forgave the members of the firing squad, and divided his gold among them. "May my blood put an end to the misfortunes of my new country," he said. "Long live Mexico!" The volley of shots shattered the silence. Maximilian murmured, *"hombre,"* and died.

Mexico, finally, was ruled by Juárez. Now, surely, he had earned the right to celebrate. But, typically, the little Indian in the worn black clothes was unable to rejoice in the way of other men. The only sign of how much his victory meant to him came on July 15, 1867, and even then only the few men who were standing next to him saw it.

On that day, Juárez entered the capital as the President of all Mexico. The crowds that lined the streets greeted him with roaring cheers. Juárez rode through the throngs, nodding gravely, a half smile on his face.

He went straight to the National Palace and climbed the stairs to the roof where, in 1862, he had lowered the flag before fleeing the French army. A little out of breath, he walked over to the flagpole. Mexico City, his capital, lay spread out before his eyes. Then he proudly raised the red, white, and green flag of Mexico. And as he did, President Benito Juárez looked up at the flag and smiled as he had never smiled before.

Reform Begins

The next day the smiles were gone. With his usual solemn manner, Juárez settled down to face the huge problem of governing Mexico. The victory over Maximilian and the French was the great turning point in Mexican history. From that time until this, no nation has tampered with Mexican independence. Without Juárez, the struggle for freedom would not have been won. But victory had come at a fearful price.

War and fighting had ripped Mexico for fifty-seven years—ever since Father Hidalgo had revolted in 1810. The long years of struggle had increased the hatred between the classes of Mexican people, a hatred that had been festering since the Age of the Conquistadores.

Most of Juárez' support had come from the mestizos, the rapidly growing class of people with both Spanish and Indian blood. The mestizos had fought savagely against the old ruling classes—the Spanish-born gachupines and the Spaniards born in Mexico known as the Creoles. The Catholic Church had sided with the Creoles and the gachupines. In the background were the five million Indians—more than twice as many people as all the other Mexicans put together. The Indians were either ignored by the other classes or used by them. Their wretched lives had not improved, despite Juárez' hopes. Most Indians still were unable to read or write. They still lived in adobe huts with dirt floors. And they still were helpless before disease.

Juárez realized that the struggle to make a united nation out of such different and embittered classes would be even harder and much longer than the fight for independence itself. The struggle would be waged in a land of such contrasts that it seems impossible that they could exist in the same country at the same time. In Mexico City, the Creole ladies still had their silk dresses and their parasols and their fine black carriages. Every day they still rode out in the late afternoon to be admired by the gentlemen. Yet a few miles from the gates of the capital, Indian fathers still carried tiny coffins to the cemeteries just as frequently as they ever had.

And throughout the land were the grim reminders of the war that had just finished. Here in a courtyard was an adobe wall riddled by the bullets of a firing squad. Here was a widow trying to raise a family by herself. Here a priest labored to rebuild a church that had been looted and burned. And everywhere, as a strange and startling backdrop to this suffering, was the magnificent beauty of Mexico. It was the wild beauty of a country that had not yet been tamed by its people—the rough beauty of the mountains and the desolate beauty of the flat, barren plains at dusk.

This was the Mexico that Juárez set out to rule in 1867 when he was re-elected President. The first problem he faced was to decide how to treat the thousands of conservatives who had fought so bitterly against him, and who still hated him. The conservative leaders were bound to be against his efforts to build a government based upon the constitution. But Juárez decided finally that there had been enough bloodshed. He pardoned the conservatives, for the most part, and allowed them to go home. Three years before, Lincoln had pardoned the Southern leaders in the same fashion.

The next problem to confront Juárez was to stay with him for the rest of his life. Mexico was nearly penniless. The years of war had drained the treasury, such as it was. Because he had no money, Juárez soon had to create another problem for himself. He quickly decided that the country could not afford to maintain the army of some sixty thousand men who had driven out the French and crushed Maximilian. He dismissed about forty thousand men from the army and thereby made nearly forty thousand enemies.

Juárez had assumed that the former soldiers would go home and work for the government. After all, they had fought for the liberals and the constitution. But these men knew no trade but war. They also had grown too fond of the power the army had given them. For years they had ruled their assigned sections of the country like little emperors. Instead of going home, many men became bandits. They seized parts of Mexico and ruled as they pleased. From time to time, the more ambitious ones would rebel against Juárez. Once attacked, the

President hunted down the bandits without mercy. But they were always turning up somewhere—raiding, robbing, and threatening to take over the government.

The violence caused by the bandits was one reason that the European nations were hesitant to put money into Mexico to help develop the country. Left on his own, Juárez did the best he could to build up the economy. He made a man named Matías Romero secretary of the treasury. Romero worked fourteen hours a day, nearly seven days a week, and he performed miracles. Slowly, a few roads began to spread throughout Mexico to tie the country together. With the help of British engineers, Juárez completed one of the most spectacular railroads in the world—a line that leaped ravines and clung to the sides of mountains and somehow made the distance of two hundred and fifty miles from Veracruz on the Gulf of Mexico to Mexico City.

Roads and trains were fine, but Juárez knew that Mexico needed educated young people even more. Schools, of course, had always been his main crusade. Some historians believe that the President's opposition to the Catholic Church came mainly from his belief that the priests had never made a real effort to educate the young people. Juárez hoped to give every Mexican child a free education. In the mid-nineteenth century, this was one of the most ambitious goals for a school system in the world. Once again, the President was held up by the lack of funds. By 1874, the system he began in 1867 had produced only eight thousand schools—enough for just three hundred and fifty thousand of Mexico's two million children.

As time went on, Juárez saw more and more clearly

101

that Mexico was really not ready to became a modern, democratic nation like the United States. Mexico had modeled its constitution after the U.S. document. The laws and the principles were there, but the country was too poor and too uneducated to put them into effect. The great mass of the Mexican people simply did not know how to take part in the life of a democracy.

Juárez also must have realized that he was rapidly running out of time to solve Mexico's problems. In 1870 he apparently suffered a slight stroke. He was sixty-four years old, a ripe age for a Mexican of that time. Juárez also felt terribly alone. Most of his old allies and friends, such as Melchor O'Campo, had been killed during the long struggle. And Juárez did not feel at ease with the young liberal leaders who were pushing their way to power in the congress.

And so a subtle change began to take place in the President of Mexico. He did not abandon his faith in the constitution, although his enemies used the freedom it gave them to attack him. He did not make himself a dictator, although he must have been sorely tempted to do so. Instead, he began to act as though he were the father of all Mexico, as though the entire country was his personal responsibility.

He began to perform, as a matter of fact, as though he were a *cacique*. In Mexico, a cacique was the most powerful man in his region of the country. He was the chief. Juárez became a kind of national cacique, the chief of all the chiefs. Although he used his power for the good of the people, he did turn many persons against him. They began whispering that he was power mad. No one

Juárez spent his life working for Mexico and its people.

likes a leader to control everything in their lives, no matter how good his intentions.

Then, in January 1871, Juárez suffered one of the gravest blows of his life. Doña Margarita, his wife, died at the age of forty-four. Juárez knew that his determination to make Mexico an independent country had helped bring about his wife's early death. Much of the time she and the children had been refugees in the United States. They lived for a while in New York City and in the nearby town of New Rochelle.

Although Juárez and his wife were often far apart, they were very close in spirit. She was twenty years younger than he, but he liked to call her "the little old lady." It was their little joke.

When Doña Margarita died, Juárez tried to hide his feelings, just as he always had done. He invited no one to the funeral. And yet the news somehow got out the day that she was buried. Crowds of people appeared at the cemetery. They stood in absolute silence, knowing without being told of the sorrow that Juárez felt.

The loss of his wife left Juárez even more isolated than ever. In 1871 he had a good chance to retire from political life. He had completed his third term as President. He was an old man. He had earned his rest. Perhaps Juárez would have acted differently if he had known that so many people feared that he wanted to stay in power forever. But, in any event, Juárez was not ready to quit. The job of binding together a nation was far from finished. He announced that he would run for a fourth term.

In those days, as we have seen, Mexico was not ready for an election as it is known in the United States today. Most of the people could not read or write. They had no idea what the constitution was or how the government worked.

These conditions were common throughout Latin America. The usual solution to the problem of governing a country was simple: the most powerful man became a dictator. This is still true today in many of the new countries of Asia and Africa, and even in some of the old countries of Latin America.

But Juárez had fought too long for the constitution to abandon it altogether. His solution was a kind of compromise. The people who were generally qualified to vote were allowed to cast ballots in the election. Juárez won, although he received less than half of the total votes cast, because there were two men running against him. A total of 5837 electors voted to give him a fourth term; 3555 voted for a man named Porfirio Díaz; and 2847 for a man named Sebastian Lerdo de Tejada. Both Díaz and Lerdo had been old friends and loyal allies of Juárez. Many liberals clearly felt that Juárez had controlled too much power for too long.

Mexican history is full of close friendships between leaders that changed to rivalries with bewildering speed. The change of heart between Benito Juárez and Porfirio Díaz is a good example. Díaz was a mestizo. He was growing up in the city of Oaxaca at the same time that Juárez was completing his education and starting his career as a young lawyer. Although Juárez was twenty-four years older than Díaz, he knew the boy. In fact, he was his teacher for a while.

Díaz grew up to be a tough and cunning soldier. He did not have Juárez' deep interest in creating a government and a constitution for Mexico, but he was a liberal and he wanted independence just as fiercely as the older man. At the age of twenty-five, Díaz had fought brilliantly against Santa Anna. He once trapped nearly a hundred conservative troops in a ravine and set an avalanche crashing down upon them.

During the war against Maximilian, Díaz had been one of Juárez' most trusted generals. He became a master of the stealthy art of striking a force that was much larger and then darting away—the type of combat now known as guerrilla warfare. Díaz knew he would have been shot if captured, and so he often did not hesitate to execute prisoners he seized himself.

Juárez came to regard his fiery general as a good fighter but an unreliable leader. The President felt that Díaz had become obsessed with killing. Juárez once reportedly said of his general, "He is a man who kills while weeping."

Because he did not trust Díaz, Juárez had made one big mistake. He treated Díaz badly right after the final defeat of Maximilian. In preparation for Juárez' triumphant return to Mexico City, Díaz had excitedly planned a great reception in the capital. He had decorated the city with flowers and banners. Díaz was also the man who remembered that Juárez would want to raise the first flag over the capital himself. He saw to it that no one else had that privilege. Then, after seeing that all was in readiness, Díaz had gone out to meet his conquering President. But Juárez had only nodded at Díaz and entered the city alone.

Later, Juárez refused to give Díaz any important post

in his new government. Angered, Díaz flatly refused to lead his troops against the rebellions staged by the liberal soldiers the President had dismissed. Díaz resigned and returned to Oaxaca to begin nursing his plans to take over the government from his old teacher.

In October 1871, after Juárez won his fourth term, Díaz struck his blow. He organized a rebellion. Many of the caciques in the mountains gave him their support. He tried to seize the government in Mexico City. But Juárez happened to have a loyal general named Sóstenes Rocha who was every bit as tough as Díaz. Rocha quickly put down the rebellion in the capital and then subdued Oaxaca. He killed Felix Díaz, the brother of Porfirio and a leader of the revolt. Porfirio Díaz himself barely escaped with his life. Disguised as a priest, he fled into the northern vastness of Mexico, just as Juárez had fled in his time.

By July 1872 Mexico was quiet again. Juárez was wearily resuming the immense task of softening the old and persisting rivalries that had split his country for so long when he suddenly felt a severe pain in his chest. He went home from work early—perhaps the only time he did so in his entire career—and allowed a doctor to look at him. During the examination, Juárez told the doctor tales of his boyhood in Oaxaca, about growing up in the city as a barefoot Indian boy who could outrun anyone on the street. Then the President abruptly asked the doctor: "Is my illness mortal?"

The doctor quietly said that he was afraid it was. Juárez then calmly continued to talk about the happy days in Oaxaca until José María Lafragua, the foreign minister, came to call. Lafragua had no idea that the President was sick, and Juárez did not want to alarm him. After carefully bracing himself in a chair, the President talked to Lafragua as usual until he left. At eleven-thirty that evening, July 18, 1872, Benito Juárez died.

ELEVEN

The Lasting Glory

For more than fifteen years, the stubborn, solemn Indian from the village of San Pablo Guelatao had been the most powerful and influential man in Mexico. Other leaders in other countries have often gained their strength by the appeal of their brilliant personalities or by the moving words they wrote. There was nothing spectacular about Juárez except his accomplishments. And while he could write a stirring speech, he did not rely upon his pen. In the end, it was Juárez' tremendous will power that made him the master of Mexico. He was absolutely determined to bring the principles of liberalism to his country.

With sheer determination, he wore down and defeated three enemies who had far more personal flair. Maximilian, of course, was captured and shot. (Carlotta, his wife, never recovered from the shock of the Emperor's defeat in Mexico. She remained insane until her death in 1927.) Napoleon III, the man who put Maximilian upon the throne, never got over the dishonor of being driven from Mexico. In 1870, seeking new honor, he marched out to fight the Germans. He was captured with an entire army. Napoleon was exiled to England, where he died in 1873. Santa Anna, the old fox, ended in complete frustration. In exile on the island of St. Thomas, he attacked "that obscure Indian, the cursed Juárez," and thought up wild schemes to carry himself back to power. None ever worked. Penniless and nearly blind, he was allowed to return to Mexico in 1874, where he died two years later at the age of eighty-two.

The one enemy that Juárez did not outlive or outlast, of course, was Porfirio Díaz, who had fled to the north in 1871. The result was a disaster for Mexico. Díaz, the brave if bloodthirsty general who had fought for liberalism, became his country's dictator. Díaz came to oppose nearly everything that Juárez had crusaded for. In many ways, Mexico stood still during Díaz' cruel reign, which was to last, with one four-year break, from 1876 until 1910.

It was Juárez' great tragedy that the problems he inherited were so great that he could not solve them in his lifetime. Juárez' great triumph was twofold. He made Mexico independent of Europe. And he gave his country the constitution and the principles and ideals it would need to become a modern nation.

Today Mexico has many of the same problems that confronted Juárez a hundred years ago. The country is still too poor. Its level of education is still too low. But Mexico is hard at work to improve the condition of its people. In many ways, the nation's goals are the same that guided Juárez a hundred years ago. This is the final and lasting glory of Benito Juárez. He had the wisdom and the courage to start his country down the long road that has led to the Mexico of today.

Index

13–15, 22, 41–42, 45–46, 67–68 (*see also* Priests, Catholic; specific individuals); Carlotta appeals to Pope for aid, 88; and class hatred, 45, 99; clergy, 61–69, 83, 84 (*see also* Priests, Catholic); and conversion of Indians, 13–15; and education, 45; Juárez and, 67–69, 99, 101; and land (property), 37, 63; Maximilian and, 83, 84, 88; and Mexican independence, 33–35, 37, 41–42; official religion in Mexico, 67–68; privileges and reforms, 22, 37, 41–42, 61–69; seminaries, 45–46; and state, separation of, 67; and struggle for control, 45

Champlain, Samuel de, 7

Chapultepec, 10; Battle of, 56

Charles IV, King, 32

Chihuahua, 68

Children: and education (schools), 23 (*see also* Education; Schools); Juárez and education of, 101; under Spanish rule, 23

Christianity (*see also* Catholic Church); conversion of Indians to, 13–15

Church. the. *See* Catholic Church; Christianity; Clergy, Catholic; Religion

Church and state, Juárez and separation of, 67–68

Ciudad Juárez, 85

Civil War, United States, 3, 77–78, 86–87

Class (classes), hatred between, 41–44, 67–68, 79, 81, 98. *See also* Creoles; Gachupines; Indians; Mestizos

Clergy, Catholic (*see also* Catholic Church; Priests); Juárez and reforms in, 61–69; Maximilian and, 83, 84

Colonialism, Spanish, 21–27, 31–38, 40–44

Colonies, North American, 6, 7, 31–32

Colorado, 49, 54

Columbus, Christopher, 7

Comanche Indians, 47

Comonfort, Ignacio, 63–64

Compostela, 15

Confederacy, U. S., *See* Civil War, United States

Congress, Mexican, 47, 72

Congress, United States, 68; Senate, 49

Conquistadores, 8–18, 20, 22

Conservatives: Juárez and, 61–69, 70–72; and Maximilian, 72, 79–89, 90–93; pardoned by Juárez, 100; and struggle for power, 44–56, 61–69

Constitution(s), Mexican, 41; of 1857, 4, 63, 64, 72, 103, 105, 106; Juárez and, 63, 64, 72, 103, 105, 106, 110

Constitution, Spanish, 41

Constitution, United States, 103

Corn, 26

Coronado, Francisco Vásquez de, 15–18, 49

Courts, Juárez and reform of, 61

Cortés, Hernán, 8–15, 18; buried in Mexico, 18; death of, 18

Coyoacán, Cortés buried in convent at, 18

Creoles, 20, 22, 26, 27, 99; and class hatred, 99; and establishment of Mexican Empire, 44; and Mexican independence, 33–38, 40–44; and struggle for power, 41–45, 99

Crockett, Davy, 49

Declaration of Independence, U. S., 31–32, 44

Degollado, Santos, 71

Degüello, 48–49

Díaz, Felix, 107

Díaz, Porfirio, 105–7; dictatorship of, 110

Diet. *See* Food (diet); specific items

Disease(s), 23, 28, 99. *See also* specific diseases

Dolores, 33, 36

Education, 7, 20, 22, 28–30, 38, 45–46, 57 (*see also* Reading, Schools); Juárez and, 101; low level of, 110

Elections, 104–5

Encomiendas, 21

England. *See* Great Britain and the British

Epidemics, 23. *See also* Disease(s)

113

69, 70–72; and Constitution of 1857, 63, 64, 72, 103, 105, 106, 110; death of daughter, 57–58; death of sons, 86; death of wife, 104; defeat and execution of Maximilian, 91–97, 98; described (appearance; characteristics; habits); 4–5, 30, 40, 51–52, 64, 65, 71, 84, 91, 96–97, 103–4, 109–10; Díaz and rebellion against, 105–7; education of, 28–30, 38, 39–40, 45–46; escapes attempt to capture him, 90; finishes college; practices law, 40, 60; forced to abandon capital by French, 76; forms constitutional government, 64–69; and French invasion of Mexico, 72–78, 79 (see also under Maximilian); as Governor of Oaxaca, 52–56, 57; helps Indians and mestizos, 57, 58; illness and death of, 102, 107–8; imprisoned in San Juan de Ulloa, 60; importance of, 4–5, 109–11; and Ley Juárez, 61–63; and Ley Lerdo, 63; marriage (wife and family), 52, 57, 60, 85–86, 104 (see also specific members); and Maximilian, 77, 79–80, 83, 84–87, 90–97, 98; as Minister of Justice (and Vice-President), 61–69; in New Orleans, 60, 61; in Oaxaca, 38, 39, 45–46, 52, 56, 57; and O'Campo, 60, 64, 70–71; as President (first term), 69, 70ff.; President again after defeat of Maximilian, 96–97, 98–108; and priesthood, 45–46; re-elected President; problems and reforms, 98–104, 110–111; and The Reform, 61–69; religion of, 45–46; and Salvanueva, 39, 45–46; and Santa Anna, 46–47, 51, 56, 57–61; saved from firing squad, 65; and Spain, 4, 6, 27; and United States, 68, 86–87, 90, 93; and War of the Reform, 64–69; wins re-election to fourth Presidential term, 105–7
Juárez, Brígida García (mother of Juárez), 3; death of, 28
Juárez, Guadalupe (daughter), 57
Juárez, Marcelino (father), 3, 28
Juárez, Margarita Maza (wife), 52, 104; death of, 104

Juárez, María Josefa (sister), 39
Justice (see also Equality); Law(s); Liberals (liberalism); Maximilian on, 83

Kansas, 15, 49, 54
Kearny, Stephen W., 55
Kings (monarchies; monarchism), 31, 44. See also specific countries, individual kings

Lafragua, José María, 107–8
Land, 3, 13, 15, 21–22 (see also Farming); Church and, 37, 63
Languages, 30
Latin America (see also South America); dictatorships in, 105
Law(s), 31, 37, 61–63; and execution of Maximilian, 93, 96; Juárez and reforms in, 61–63; Maximilian and, 83, 84; under Spanish rule, 22
Lee, Robert E., 55, 86
Lempriere, Charles, 71
Lerdo de Tejada, Sebastian, 105
Ley Juárez, 61–63
Ley Lerdo, 63
Liberals (liberalism); and independence, 31–32, 41–42; Juárez and, 56, 60–69, 70–72, 76, 85–89, 90ff., 103, 105–7, 109; Maximilian and, 77, 83; and struggle for control, 44–56, 60–69
Lincoln, Abraham, 78, 100; assassinated; succeeded by Johnson, 86–87; and French invasion of Mexico, 78, 86
Locke, John, on equality and natural rights, 30–31
Louis Napoleon. See Napoleon III (Louis Napoleon)

Manifest Destiny, United States policy of, 52, 56, 68
Marriage (intermarriage), 26–27, 52. See also Indians, Mexican, Mestizos
Maximilian, Emperor, 77–78, 79–89, 90–97, 98, 106; and the Church, 83, 84, 88; and court etiquette, 78, 81, 91, 93; described, 81, 82, 91–92, 96; end of his em-

115

pire, 86–89, 90–97, 98; Juárez and, 77, 79–80, 83, 84–87, 90–97, 98; liberalism and reforms of, 77, 83–84, 96; plans Mexican navy, 81; portraits of, 81, 82; Querétaro defeat, 90–93; trial and execution of, 93–96; United States and, 73, 86–87, 90, 93

Maza, Antonio, 39, 52

Maza, Margarita. *See* Juárez, Margarita Maza

Mestizos, 26–27, 32; and class hatred, 26–27, 44–45, 98–99; Juárez and reforms, 57, 58, 98–99; and Mexican independence, 32–38, 40, 41–44; result of intermarriage between Indians and Spanish, 26–27; and struggle for power, 26–27, 44–45, 98–99

Mexican Empire, Creoles and creation of, 44

Mexican War, 52–56

Mexico, beauty and description of, 3, 81, 99–100. *See also* specific locations

Mexico, Valley of (Anáhuac), 9, 11, 81

Mexico City, 9; Cathedral in, 22, 50, 80; described at time of American Revolution, 26; Juárez in as President, 69–78; Juárez re-enters as President after defeat of Maximilian, 96–97, 106; Maximilian in, 80; in Mexican War, 55, 56; National Palace in, 97; Rocha subdues Díaz rebellion in, 107; Santa Anna reappears in, 57

Mines and mining, 20, 22. *See also* Gold; Silver

Miramón, Miguel, as conservative general, 91; as conservative President, 69

Moctezuma, (Emperor of the Aztecs), 10–12, 15; stoning and death of, 12

Monroe Doctrine, 44, 45, 73, 86–87; declaration by President James Monroe of, 44; and French in Mexico, 73, 86–87, 90

Monroe, James, 44. *See also* Monroe Doctrine

Mora, José María Luis, 60

Morelos, José María, 37–38, 40, 41,

61; Alvarez and, 61; execution of, 37, 41; fights for equality, 37–38, 40; Juárez and, 38

Mountains, 3, 81, 99

Napoleon Bonaparte (Napoleon I), 32, 73; and invasion of Spain, 32; Santa Anna compares himself to, 50

Napoleon III (Louis Napoleon), 72–76, 78, 86–87; defeat and death of, 110; and invasion of Mexico, 72–76, 86–87; refuses aid to Maximilian and Carlotta, 88

Natural rights (*see also* Equality); Justice; Liberals (liberalism); John Locke on, 30–31

Nevada, 54

New Mexico, 15, 49, 68

New Orleans, La., Juárez in exile in, 60–61

Nobility, the, 31. *See also* Ruling classes

Noche triste, la, 12

Nueces River, 54

Oaxaca (city), 38, 45–46, 105, 107

Oaxaca (state), 1, 15, 45–46, 51, 52; Cortés given huge grants in, 15; Juárez as governor of, 52, 56, 57–60

O'Campo, Melchor, 60, 64, 103; captured by conservatives and executed, 70–71; Juárez and, 60, 64, 70–71, 103

Oregon, 56

Ortega, González, 69

Pacific Ocean and coast, United States foreign policy and, 52–56

"Pastry war," 50

Petate, 23

Peonage (*see also* Slave labor); abolished by Maximilian, 84

Polk, James Knox, 52–56; and United States Manifest Destiny policy, 52–56

Presidents (presidency), Mexican, 47, 50–51. *See also* specific individuals

Priests, Aztec, 10, 11

Priests, Catholic, 13–15, 22, 45–46, 61–69, 83, 84 (*see also* Catholic

Church; Clergy, Catholic; specific individuals); and independence, 33–35 (*see also* specific priests); Juárez and, 101
Prieto, Guillermo, 65
Pronunciamiento, 50–51
Prussia, 40, 88

Querétaro, Battle of, 91–93

Railroads, 101
Ranches, 20, 22
Reactionaries, 45, 76. *See also* Conservatives
Reading, 30, 99, 105. *See also* Education
Reform, The, 4, 61–69, 83–84
Religion (*see also* Catholic Church; Christianity); Aztec, 10, 13–15; Juárez and, 45–46, 67–68
Río Grande River, 54–55, 56
Roads (road-building), 101
Roman Catholicism. *See* Catholic Church
Rocha, Sóstenes, 107
Romero, Matías, 101
Ruling classes, 31, 45, 98–99 (*see also* Creoles; Gachupines), *pronunciamiento* and, 50–51

Sacrifice(s), Aztec, 10, 13
St. Thomas, Santa Anna in exile on island of, 110
Salamanca, Battle of, 65
Salanueva, Antonio, 39, 45–46; adopts Juárez and agrees to educate him, 39, 45–46
San Antonio, Texas, United States and Mexican battle at, 48–49
San Jacinto, Battle of, 49
San Juan de Ulloa, Juárez imprisoned in, 60
San Martín, José de, 32, 41
San Pablo Guelatao, 1–5, 28, 30
Santa Anna, Antonio López de, 46–61, 76, 106; "Age of," 50–56; death of, 110; described, 46–47, 61; as dictator, 47–51, 61; Juárez and, 46–47, 51, 56, 57–61; and Mexican War with U.S., 55–56; overthrown and exiled, 61, 72, 110; and Texas dispute, 42, 49; and war with France, 49–50

Santo Tomás Ixtlán (church), 4
Schools (school system), 23, 45–46, 83, 101 (*see also* Education); Juárez and, 101; Maximilian and, 83
Scott, Winfield, 55
Seminaries, Catholic, 45–46
Senate, United States, 49
Sheridan, Philip, 86–87
Sickness. *See* Disease(s)
Sierra, Justo, 38
Silver, 11, 12, 13, 22, 26
Slave labor, under Spanish rule, 21–22. *See also* Peonage; Slaves and slavery
Slaves and slavery, 10. *See also* Slave labor; Peonage
Slidell, John, 54, 77–78
Smallpox, 23
Sonora, 68
South America, 32, 41, 44; struggle for independence in, 32, 41 (*see also* Europe; specific countries); United States and Monroe Doctrine, 44 (*see also* Monroe Doctrine)
Spain and the Spaniards, 4, 6–18, 32, 98–99 (*see also* specific individuals); and colonialism, 6–18, 21–27, 31–38, 40–44; conquest of Mexico by, 7–18; control of Mexico by, 6–18, 19–27, 31–38, 40–44; and Mexican debt, 22, 74–76; and Mexican independence, 32–38, 40–44, 72, 74–76; Napoleon and, 32, 40; revolt and granting of constitution in, 40–41; War of Independence against, 33–38, 40–44

Taxes, 22
Taylor, Zachary, 54–55
Temples, Aztec, 10
Tenochtitlán, 9–12, 13, 26; description of, 9–10; siege of, 13
Texas, 47–49; annexed by United States, 49, 52, 54; Mexican War and, 47–49; Republic of, 49
Texcoco, Lake, 9–10
Tlaxcala, 12
Trains (railroad construction), 101

United States, 31–32, 68 (*see also* specific individuals, places); and aid to Juárez, 86, 87, 90, 93; American Revolution, 6, 32, 44; Civil War in, 73, 77–78, 86–87; colonial era and independence of, 6, 7, 31–32, 44; Congress, 49, 68; Declaration of Independence, 44; and French invasion of Mexico, 73, 77–78, 86–87, 90, 93; Juárez and fear of seizure of territory in Mexico by, 68; and Manifest Destiny, 52–56, 68; Mexico and foreign policy of, 44, 45, 47–49, 52–56, 68, 73, 86–87; and Mexican War, 52–56; and Monroe Doctrine, 44, 45, 73, 86–87; and Texas dispute, 47–49, 52, 54

Utah, 54

Urrea, General, 51

Valle, Leandro, 71

Valley of Mexico. *See* Mexico, Valley of (Anáhuac)

Veracruz, 50, 55; Juárez in, 67–69; Maximilian and Carlotta arrive in, 78

Viceroy, office of, 20, 21

Vicksburg, Battle, 77

Victoria, Guadalupe, as Mexico's first President, 47

Virginia, English settlement in, 7

War of Independence, Mexican, 33–38, 40–44

War of the Reform, 4, 64–69

Water supply, Aztec, 10

Wyoming, 49

Yucatán, 9, 10–11

Zacatecas, 90

Zapotec language, 30